*When you gave your heart to Christ,*
*you inherited a great wealth—*
*all the hundreds of promises*
*God gave you in His Word.*
*These promises rightfully belong*
*to you as a child of God.*
*You must claim them, believe*
*them and act upon them.*

*"Whereby are given unto
us exceeding great and
precious promises:
that by these ye might be
partakers of the divine nature."*
2 Peter 1:4 (KJV)

# the Jesus Person Pocket Promise Book

## David Wilkerson

**Chosen**

a division of Baker Publishing Group
Minneapolis, Minnesota

© 1972 by Regal Books

Published by Chosen Books
11400 Hampshire Avenue South
Bloomington, Minnesota 55438
www.chosenbooks.com

Chosen Books is a division of
Baker Publishing Group, Grand Rapids, Michigan

Chosen Books edition published 2014
ISBN 978-0-8007-9757-7

Previously published by Regal Books, originally as *Promises to
Live by...The Pocket Promise Book*

Printed in the United States of America

Library of Congress Catalog Card No. 71-86208
ISBN 0-8307-0191-5

19  20  21  22  23  24        10  9  8  7  6  5

## GOD'S PROMISES FOR YOUR SPIRITUAL NEEDS

A. The blood of Jesus Christ cleanses you from sin. **1—20**

B. Jesus Christ died to give you eternal life. **21—43**

C. You can expect His presence in your life. **44—57**

D. You can expect answers to your prayers. **58—83**

E. God will keep you. **84—107**

F. God will give you strength for His service. **108—124**

G. God will teach you truth. **125—143**

H. God will work miracles in your life. **144—152**

I. God will fill your life with love. **153—169**

J. You can grow spiritually. **170—180**

K. The Lord will baptize you in the Holy Spirit. **181—200**

L. God will give you a new freedom. **201—209**

M. God instills faith in you. **210—241**

N. Jesus Christ forgives your daily sins. **242—254**

O. The Lord brings hope to you. **255—269**

P. The Word of God is alive. **270—289**

Q. God honors obedience. **290—315**

R. God leaves surrender up to you. **316—328**

S. God honors holiness. **329—349**

T. God blesses clean conversation. **350—371**

U. God will bless your family. **372—382**

# How to Make These Promises Work in Your Life

When you gave your heart to Christ and became a Jesus person, you inherited a great wealth—all the hundreds of promises God gave you in His Word.

These promises rightfully belong to you as a child of God. You must claim them, believe them and act upon them. Here's how:

1. Take each promise to mean just exactly what it says. Don't try to interpret it or add to it or read between the lines. Accept it literally.

2. Get your mind and heart in condition to believe the promises. God's Word says, "If I regard iniquity in my heart, the Lord will not hear me" (Psalm 66:18). Be sure there is no sin in your life. If there is some sin (hatred, bitterness, jealousy, lust, for example), ask the Lord for His forgiveness. Pray to have your mind renewed in the Holy Ghost.

3. If there is a part of the promise which depends upon your action, you must be willing to do it—follow through. If it says "pray," then pray. If it next says "believe," then you must believe in order to expect God to act. God is ready to do His part. You must be ready also to do yours.

4. Now, after you have done these first three things, you must be willing to wait on the Lord's time in answering. The promised answer may come immediately. Then again—it may not. Just don't get uptight! God *will* keep His promise. If the answer is long in coming, you can remember that He has a perfect time and a perfect plan for your life. Meanwhile, you might read the promise section on "Patience."

Follow these four steps to claiming all the promises God has given you to use. Take time to read some of them in your Bible in the context of the whole chapter where it appears. If you find one verse especially helpful, memorize it. Then you'll have it at your fingertips. Always remember that whatever God said—He will do!

Carry this book with you at all times. Think of it as a Bible promise dictionary and refer to it for answers to all your questions and needs. Memorize *all* the key verses and use them daily to open God's storehouse of benefits. God cannot and will not break one of these promises. Every promise in this book is yours! Trust them—stand on them—believe them. Then you can say, "God said it—I believe it—that settles it."

*"Being fully persuaded*
*that, what he had promised,*
*he was able also to perform."*
Romans 4:21 (KJV)

# GOD'S PROMISES FOR YOUR SPIRITUAL NEEDS

## A. The blood of Jesus Christ cleanses you from sin.

**KEY VERSE: 1.** *The blood of Jesus His Son cleanses us from all sin.* I John 1:7 NASB

**2.** In whom we have redemption through his blood, even the forgiveness of sins. Colossians 1:14 KJV

**3.** He shall save his people from their sins. Matthew 1:21 KJV

**4.** Who gave himself for our sins. Galatians 1:4 KJV

**5.** If we confess our sins, he is faithful and just to forgive us our sins, and to cleanse us from all unrighteousness. I John 1:9 KJV

**6.** For this is my blood of the covenant, which is to be shed on behalf of many for forgiveness of sins. Matthew 26:28 NASB

**7.** Behold, the Lamb of God who takes away the sin of the world. John 1:29 NASB

**8.** But he was wounded and bruised for our sins. He was chastised that we might have peace; he was lashed—and we were healed. Isaiah 53:5 LB

**9.** Without the shedding of blood there is no forgiveness of sins. Hebrews 9:22 LB

**10.** In whom we have redemption through his blood, the forgiveness of sins, according to the riches of his grace. Ephesians 1:7 KJV

**11.** And he himself bore our sins in his body on the cross, that we might die to sin and live to righteousness; for by his wounds you were healed. I Peter 2:24 NASB

**12.** Neither by the blood of goats and calves, but by his own blood he entered in once into the holy place, having obtained eternal redemption for us. Hebrews 9:12 KJV

**13.** To him who loves us, and releases us from our sins by his blood. Revelation 1:5 NASB

**14.** The blood of Christ, who through the eternal Spirit offered himself without blemish to God, cleanse your conscience from dead works to serve the living God. Hebrews 9:14 NASB

**15.** But now in Christ Jesus you who formerly were far off have been brought near by the blood of Christ. Ephesians 2:13 NASB

**16.** Knowing that you were not redeemed with perishable things like silver or gold from your futile way of life inherited from your forefathers, but with precious blood, as of a lamb unblemished and spotless, the blood of Christ. I Peter 1:18,19 NASB

**17.** And since by his blood he did all this for us as sinners, how much more will he do for us now that he has declared us not guilty? Now he will save us from all of God's wrath to come. Romans 5:9 LB

**18.** For Christ's death on the cross has made peace with God for all by his blood. Colossians 1:20 LB

**19.** Christ came at just the right time and died for us sinners who had no use for him. Romans 5:6 LB

**20.** But God showed his great love for us by sending Christ to die for us while we were still sinners. Romans 5:8 LB

# B. Jesus Christ died to give you eternal life.

**KEY VERSE: 21.** *For God so loved the world, that he gave his only begotten Son, that whoever believes in him should not perish, but have eternal life.* John 3:16 NASB

**22.** Truly, truly I say to you, he who believes has eternal life. John 6:47 NASB

**23.** The wages of sin is death; but the gift of God is eternal life through Jesus Christ our Lord. Romans 6:23 KJV

**24.** I say emphatically that anyone who listens to my message and believes in God who sent me has eternal life, and will never be damned for his sins, but has already passed out of death into life. John 5:24 LB

**25.** And this is life eternal, that they might know thee, the only true God, and Jesus Christ whom thou hast sent. John 17:3 KJV

**26.** And this is the promise which he himself made to us, the eternal life. I John 2:25 NASB

**27.** This is the bread which came down out of heaven; not as the fathers ate, and died; he who eats this bread shall live forever. John 6:58 NASB

**28.** My sheep hear my voice, and I know them, and they follow me: and I give unto them eternal life: and they shall never perish, neither shall any man pluck them out of my hand. John 10:27,28 KJV

**29.** And the witness is this, that God has given us eternal life, and this life is in his Son. I John 5:11 NASB

**30.** These things I have written to you who believe in the name of the Son of God, in order that you may know that you have eternal life. I John 5:13 NASB

**31.** In hope of eternal life, which God, that cannot lie, promised before the world began. Titus 1:2 KJV

**32.** God will redeem my soul from the power of the grave: for he shall receive me.   Psalm 49:15 KJV

**33.** If the Spirit of him who raised Jesus from the dead dwells in you, he who raised Christ Jesus from the dead will also give life to your mortal bodies through his Spirit who indwells you.   Romans 8:11 NASB

**34.** I am the resurrection and the life; he who believes in me shall live even if he dies.   John 11:25 NASB

**35.** He who raised the Lord Jesus will raise us also with Jesus and will present us with you.   II Corinthians 4:14 NASB

**36.** Since we believe that Jesus died and then came back to life again, we can also believe that when Jesus returns, God will bring back with him all the Christians who have died.   I Thessalonians 4:14 LB

**37.** And now he has made all of this plain to us by the coming of our Savior Jesus Christ, who broke the power of death and showed us the way of everlasting life through trusting him.   II Timothy 1:10 LB

**38.** We shall be saved by his life. Those who receive the abundance of grace and of the gift of righteousness will reign in life through the one, Jesus Christ.   Romans 5:10,17 NASB

**39.** The gift of God is eternal life through Jesus Christ our Lord.   Romans 6:23 KJV

**40.** Christ came with this new agreement so that all who are invited may come and have forever all the wonders God has promised them. For Christ died to rescue them from the penalty of the sins they had committed while still under that old system.   Hebrews 9:15 LB

**41.** The one who sows to his own flesh shall from the flesh reap corruption, but the one who sows to the Spirit shall from the Spirit reap eternal life.   Galatians 6:8 NASB

**42.** That being justified by his grace we might be made

heirs according to the hope of eternal life.   Titus 3:7
NASB

**43.** O death, where is your victory? O death, where
is your sting? Thanks be to God, who gives us the victory through our Lord Jesus Christ.   I Corinthians
15:55,57 NASB

# C. You can expect His presence in your life.

**KEY VERSE: 44.** *My presence shall go with you, and
I will give you rest. Exodus 33:14 NASB*

**45.** The upright will dwell in thy presence. Psalm
140:13 NASB

**46.** The Lord is with you when you are with him. And
if you seek him, he will let you find him.   II Chronicles
15:2 NASB

**47.** The Lord is the one who goes ahead of you; he
will be with you. He will not fail you or forsake you.
Do not fear, or be dismayed. Deuteronomy 31:8
NASB

**48.** And be sure of this—that I am with you always,
even to the end of the world.   Matthew 28:20 LB

**49.** I am the vine, you are the branches; he who abides
in me, and I in him, he bears much fruit; for apart from
me you can do nothing.   John 15:5 NASB

**50.** If a man love me, he will keep my words: and
my Father will love him, and we will come unto him,
and make our abode with him.   John 14:23 KJV

**51.** I am the Lord your God, and none else: and my
people shall never be ashamed.   Joel 2:27 KJV

**52.** The Lord has set apart the godly man for himself.   Psalm 4:3 NASB

**53.** The Lord loves the righteous.   Psalm 146:8 NASB

**54.** Look! I have been standing at the door and I am constantly knocking. If anyone hears me calling him and opens the door, I will come in and fellowship with him and he with me.   Revelation 3:20 LB

**55.** The Lord God is a sun and shield; the Lord will give grace and glory; no good thing will he withhold from them that walk uprightly.   Psalm 84:11 KJV

**56.** Salvation belongs to the Lord; thy blessing be upon thy people.   Psalm 3:8 NASB

**57.** For as many as are led by the Spirit of God, they are sons of God.   Romans 8:14 KJV

# D. You can expect answers to your prayers.

**KEY VERSE: 58.** *If you abide in me, and my words abide in you, ask whatever you wish, and it will be done for you.*   John 15:7 NASB

**59.** Therefore I say to you, all things for which you pray and ask, believe that you have received them, and they shall be granted you.   Mark 11:24 NASB

**60.** Thou hast given him his heart's desire, and thou hast not withheld the request of his lips.   Psalm 21:2 NASB

**61.** We know that all things work together for good to them that love God, to them who are the called according to his purpose.   Romans 8:28 KJV

**62.** Yes, the Lord hears the good man when he calls to him for help, and saves him out of all his troubles. Psalm 34:17 LB

**63.** Be delighted with the Lord. Then he will give you all your heart's desires.   Psalm 37:4 LB

**64.** Call upon me in the day of trouble; I shall rescue you, and you will honor me.   Psalm 50:15 NASB

**65.** As for me, I will call upon God; and the Lord shall save me.   Psalm 55:16 KJV

**66.** Evening, and morning, and at noon, will I pray, and cry aloud: and he shall hear my voice.   Psalm 55:17 KJV

**67.** In the day of my trouble I shall call upon thee, for thou wilt answer me.   Psalm 86:7 NASB

**68.** Ask, and it shall be given to you; seek, and you shall find; knock, and it shall be opened to you.   Matthew 7:7 NASB

**69.** It shall come to pass, that before they call, I will answer; and while they are yet speaking, I will hear.   Isaiah 65:24 KJV

**70.** Call to me, and I will answer you, and I will tell you great and mighty things, which you do not know.   Jeremiah 33:3 NASB

**71.** Then you will call, and the Lord will answer; You will cry, and he will say, Here am I.   Isaiah 58:9 NASB

**72.** Yes, ask anything, using my name, and I will do it.   John 14:14 LB

**73.** He shall call upon me, and I will answer him: I will be with him in trouble; I will deliver him, and honor him.   Psalm 91:15 KJV

**74.** Whatsoever we ask, we receive of him, because we keep his commandments, and do those things that are pleasing in his sight.   I John 3:22 KJV

**75.** Again I say unto you, That if two of you shall agree on earth as touching anything that they shall ask, it shall be done for them of my Father which is in heaven.   Matthew 18:19 KJV

**76.** If my people, which are called by my name, shall humble themselves, and pray, and seek my face, and turn from their wicked ways; then will I hear from heaven, and will forgive their sin, and will heal their land.   II Chronicles 7:14 KJV

**77.** And everything you ask in prayer, believing, you shall receive.   Matthew 21:22 NASB

**78.** Everyone who asks receives; and he who seeks finds; and to him who knocks it shall be opened.   Luke 11:10 NASB

**79.** This is the confidence which we have before him, that, if we ask anything according to his will, he hears us.   I John 5:14 NASB

**80.** And if we know that he hears us in whatever we ask, we know that we have the requests which we have asked from him.   I John 5:15 NASB

**81.** Since he did not spare even his own Son for us but gave him up for us all, won't he also surely give us everything else?   Romans 8:32 LB

**82.** Commit your way to the Lord, trust also in him, and he will do it.   Psalm 37:5 NASB

**83.** He is a rewarder of them that diligently seek him.   Hebrews 11:6 KJV


# E. God will keep you.

**KEY VERSE: 84.** *Holy Father, keep through thine own name those whom thou hast given me.   John 17:11 KJV*

**85.** But the Lord is faithful, and he will strengthen and protect you from the evil one.   II Thessalonians 3:3 NASB

**86.** My Father, who has given them to me, is greater than all; and no one is able to snatch them out of the Father's hand.   John 10:29 NASB

**87.** He who establishes us with you in Christ and anointed us is God.   II Corinthians 1:21 NASB

**88.** Who shall also confirm you to the end, blameless in the day of our Lord Jesus Christ.   I Corinthians 1:8 NASB

**89.** Being confident of this very thing, that he which hath begun a good work in you will perform it until the day of Jesus Christ.   Philippians 1:6 KJV

**90.** I am persuaded, that neither death, nor life, nor angels, nor principalities, nor powers, nor things present, nor things to come, nor height, nor depth, nor any other creature, shall be able to separate us from the love of God, which is in Christ Jesus our Lord.   Romans 8:38,39 KJV

**91.** The righteous is an everlasting foundation.   Proverbs 10:25 KJV

**92.** If I should say "My foot has slipped," thy loving-kindness, O Lord, will hold me up.   Psalm 94:18 NASB

**93.** Who are kept by the power of God through faith unto salvation.   I Peter 1:5 KJV

**94.** Unto him that is able to keep you from falling, and to present you faultless before the presence of his glory with exceeding joy.   Jude 24 KJV

**95.** Be all the more diligent to make certain about his calling and choosing you; for as long as you practice these things, you will never stumble.   II Peter 1:10 NASB

**96.** No one who has become part of God's family makes a practice of sinning, for Christ, God's Son, holds him securely and the devil cannot get his hands on him.   I John 5:18 LB

**97.** God himself shall be with them, and be their God.   Revelation 21:3 KJV

**98.** You shall be my people and I will be your God.   Jeremiah 30:22 LB

**99.** I will be their God, and they shall be my people.   II Corinthians 6:16 KJV

**100.** God is not ashamed to be called their God, for he has made a heavenly city for them.   Hebrews 11:16 LB

**101.** He shall feed his flock like a shepherd: he shall gather the lambs in his arm, and carry them in his bosom, and shall gently lead those that are with young.   Isaiah 40:11 KJV

**102.** Though I am surrounded by troubles, you will bring me safely through them. You will clench your fist against my angry enemies! Your power will save me.   Psalm 138:7 LB

**103.** The Lord will be your confidence, and will keep your foot from being caught.   Proverbs 3:26 NASB

**104.** The angel of the Lord encamps around those who fear him, and rescues them.   Psalm 34:7 NASB

**105.** I have set the Lord always before me; because he is at my right hand, I shall not be moved.   Psalm 16:8 KJV

**106.** He is always watching, never sleeping. Jehovah himself is caring for you.   Psalm 121:4,5 LB

**107.** You are my hiding place from every storm of life; you even keep me from getting into trouble! You surround me with songs of victory.   Psalm 32:7 LB

# F. God will give you strength for His service.

**KEY VERSE: 108:** *Not by might, nor by power, but by my Spirit, says the Lord of Hosts.   Zechariah 4:6 LB*

**109.** The God of Israel gives strength and mighty power to his people.   Psalm 68:35 LB

**110.**   You shall receive power when the Holy Spirit has come upon you; and you shall be my witnesses both in Jerusalem, and in all Judea and Samaria, and even to the remotest part of the earth.   Acts 1:8 NASB

**111.** Trust in the Lord God always, for in the Lord Jehovah is your everlasting strength.   Isaiah 26:4 LB

**112.** But as many as received him, to them he gave

the right to become children of God, even to those who believe in his name.   John 1:12 NASB

**113.** They that wait upon the Lord shall renew their strength; they shall mount up with wings as eagles; they shall run, and not be weary: and they shall walk, and not faint.   Isaiah 40:31 KJV

**114.** And he said unto me, My grace is sufficient for thee: for my strength is made perfect in weakness.   II Corinthians 12:9 KJV

**115.** So use every piece of God's armor to resist the enemy whenever he attacks, and when it is all over, you will still be standing up.   Ephesians 6:13 LB

**116.** Do not fear, for I am with you; do not anxiously look about you, for I am your God. I will strengthen you, surely I will help you, surely I will uphold you with my righteous right hand.   Isaiah 41:10 NASB

**117.** For God is at work within you, helping you want to obey him, and then helping you do what he wants.   Philippians 2:13 LB

**118.** But the salvation of the righteous is of the Lord; he is their strength in the time of trouble.   Psalm 37:39 KJV

**119.** That he would grant you, according to the riches of his glory, to be strengthened with might by his Spirit in the inner man.   Ephesians 3:16 KJV

**120.** I can do all things through him who strengthens me.   Philippians 4:13 NASB

**121.** We are praying, too, that you will be filled with his mighty, glorious strength so that you can keep going no matter what happens—always full of the joy of the Lord.   Colossians 1:11 LB

**122.** The righteous shall move onward and forward; those with pure hearts shall become stronger and stronger.   Job 17:9 LB

**123.** For we are his workmanship, created in Christ Jesus for good works, which God prepared beforehand, that we should walk in them.   Ephesians 2:10 NASB

**124.** I will lift up my eyes to the mountains; from whence shall my help come? My help comes from the Lord, who made heaven and earth.   Psalm 121:1,2 NASB

# G. God will teach you truth.

**KEY VERSE: 125.** *I will instruct you (says the Lord) and guide you along the best pathway for your life; I will advise you and watch your progress. Psalm 32:8 LB*

**126.** He knows just what to do, for God has made him see and understand.   Isaiah 28:26 LB

**127.** For God, who said, "Light shall shine out of darkness," is the One who has shone in our hearts to give the light of the knowledge of the glory of God in the face of Christ.   II Corinthians 4:6 NASB

**128.** Come let us go up the mountain of the Lord, to the Temple of the God of Israel; there he will teach us his laws, and we will obey them.   Isaiah 2:3 LB

**129.** Where is the man who fears the Lord? God will teach him how to choose the best.   Psalm 25:12 LB

**130.** If any man will do his will, he shall know of the doctrine, whether it be of God, or whether I speak of myself.   John 7:17 KJV

**131.** He encircled him, he cared for him, he guarded him as the pupil of his eye.   Deuteronomy 32:10 NASB

**132.** That the God of our Lord Jesus Christ, the Father of glory, may give unto you the spirit of wisdom and revelation in the knowledge of him.   Ephesians 1:17 KJV

**133.** But when he, the Spirit of truth, comes, he will guide you into all the truth; for he will not speak on his own initiative, but whatever he hears, he will speak; and he will disclose to you what is to come.    John 16:13 NASB

**134.** The secret things belong unto the Lord our God: but those things which are revealed belong unto us and to our children forever, that we may do all the words of this law.    Deuteronomy 29:29 KJV

**135.** All things that I have heard of my Father I have made known unto you.    John 15:15 KJV

**136.** No mere man has ever seen, heard or even imagined what wonderful things God has ready for those who love the Lord. But we know about these things because God has sent his Spirit to tell us, and his Spirit searches out and shows us all of God's deepest secrets.    I Corinthians 2:9,10 LB

**137.** He reveals profound mysteries beyond man's understanding. He knows all hidden things, for he is light, and darkness is no obstacle to him.    Daniel 2:22 LB

**138.** Behold, the former things are come to pass, and new things do I declare. Before they spring forth I tell you of them.    Isaiah 42:9 KJV

**139.** For now we see in a mirror dimly, but then face to face; now I know in part, but then I shall know fully just as I also have been fully known.    I Corinthians 13:12 NASB

**140.** As it is written in the Scriptures, They shall all be taught of God. Those the Father speaks to, who learn the truth from him, will be attracted to me.    John 6:45 LB

**141.** The Comforter, which is the Holy Ghost, whom the Father will send in my name, he shall teach you all things, and bring all things to your remembrance, whatsoever I have said unto you.    John 14:26 KJV

**142.** From a wise mind comes careful and persuasive speech.    Proverbs 16:23 LB

**143.** The meek will he guide in judgment: and the meek will he teach his way.   Psalm 25:9 KJV

# H. God will work miracles in your life.

**KEY VERSE: 144.** *If you can! All things are possible to him who believes.   Mark 9:23 NASB*

**145.** Truly, truly, I say to you, he who believes in me, the works that I do shall he do also; and greater works than these shall he do; because I go to the Father.   John 14:12 NASB

**146.** Whatever you ask in my name, that will I do, that the Father may be glorified in the Son.   John 14:13 NASB

**147.** Yes, ask anything, using my name, and I will do it.   John 14:14 LB

**148.** Now to him who is able to do exceeding abundantly beyond all that we ask or think, according to the power that works within us.   Ephesians 3:20 NASB

**149.** If you had faith even as small as a tiny mustard seed nothing would be impossible.   Matthew 17:20 LB

**150.** If two of you shall agree on earth as touching any thing that they shall ask, it shall be done for them of my Father which is in heaven.   Matthew 18:19 KJV

**151.** God has appointed in the church, first apostles, second prophets, third teachers, then miracles, then gifts of healings, helps, administrations, various kinds of tongues.   I Corinthians 12:28 NASB

**152.** To another the working of miracles; to another prophecy; to another discerning of spirits; to another divers kinds of tongues; to another the interpretation of tongues.   I Corinthians 12:10 KJV

# I. God will fill your life with love.

**KEY VERSE: 153.** *We have come to know and have believed the love which God has for us. God is love, and the one who abides in love abides in God, and God abides in him.  1 John 4:16 NASB*

**154.** If you keep my commandments, you will abide in my love; just as I have kept my Father's commandments, and abide in his love.  John 15:10 NASB

**155.** Hatred stirs old quarrels, but love overlooks insults.  Proverbs 10:12 LB

**156.** The Lord keeps all who love him; but all the wicked he will destroy.  Psalm 145:20 NASB

**157.** The one who obeys me is the one who loves me; and because he loves me, my Father will love him; and I will too, and I will reveal myself to him.  John 14:21 LB

**158.** The person who truly loves God is the one who is open to God's knowledge.  I Corinthians 8:3 LB

**159.** As the Father has loved me, I have also loved you; abide in My love.  John 15:9 NASB

**160.** To love him with all the heart, and with all the understanding, and with all the soul, and with all the strength, and to love his neighbor as himself; is more than all whole burnt offerings and sacrifices.  Mark 12:33 KJV

**161.** Things which eye has not seen and ear has not heard, and which have not entered the heart of man, all that God has prepared for those who love him.  I Corinthians 2:9 NASB

**162.** To know the love of Christ which surpasses knowledge, that you may be filled up to all the fulness of God.  Ephesians 3:19 NASB

**163.** In this act we see what real love is; it is not our love for God, but his love for us when he sent his Son

15

to satisfy God's anger against our sins. I John 4:10 LB

**164.** Beloved, let us love one another, for love is from God, and every one who loves is born of God and knows God. I John 4:7 NASB

**165.** Nor height, nor depth, nor any other created thing, shall be able to separate us from the love of God, which is in Christ Jesus our Lord. Romans 8:39 NASB

**166.** Though we have never yet seen God, when we love each other God lives in us and his love within us grows ever stronger. I John 4:12 LB

**167.** We need have no fear of someone who loves us perfectly; his perfect love for us eliminates all dread of what he might do to us. If we are afraid, it is for fear of what he might do to us, and shows that we are not fully convinced that he really loves us. I John 4:18 LB

**168.** I love them that love me; and those that seek me early shall find me. Proverbs 8:17 KJV

**169.** There are three things that remain—faith, hope, and love—and the greatest of these is love. I Corinthians 13:13 LB

## J. You can grow spiritually.

**KEY VERSE: 170.** *But we all, with unveiled face beholding as in a mirror the glory of the Lord, are being transformed into the same image from glory to glory, just as from the Lord, the Spirit. II Corinthians 3:18 NASB*

**171.** That Christ will be more and more at home in your hearts, living within you as you trust in him. May your roots go down deep into the soil of God's marvelous love; and may you be able to feel and understand, as all God's children should, how long, how wide, how deep, and how high his love really is; and to experience this love for yourselves, though it is so great that you will never see the end of it or fully know or understand it. And so at last you will be filled up with God himself. Ephesians 3:17-19 LB

**172.** The righteous shall flourish like the palm tree: he shall grow like a cedar in Lebanon. Psalm 92:12 KJV

**173.** Like newborn babes, long for the pure milk of the word, that by it you may grow in respect to salvation, if you have tasted the kindness of the Lord. I Peter 2:2,3 NASB

**174.** The path of the righteous is like the light of dawn, that shines brighter and brighter until the full day. Proverbs 4:18 NASB

**175.** He humbled you by letting you go hungry and then feeding you with manna, a food previously unknown to both you and your ancestors. He did it to help you realize that food isn't everything, and that real life comes by obeying every command of God. Deuteronomy 8:3 LB

**176.** For I am confident of this very thing, that he who began a good work in you will perfect it until the day of Christ Jesus. Philippians 1:6 NASB

**177.** Be no more children, tossed to and fro, and carried about with every wind of doctrine, by the sleight of man, and cunning craftiness, whereby they lie in wait to deceive; but speaking the truth in love, may grow up into him in all things, which is the head, even Christ. Ephesians 4:14,15 KJV

**178.** That you may walk in a manner worthy of the Lord, to please him in all respects, bearing fruit in every good work and increasing in the knowledge of God. Colossians 1:10 NASB

**179.** My prayer for you is that you will overflow more

and more with love for others, and at the same time keep on growing in spiritual knowledge and insight, for I want you always to see clearly the difference between right and wrong, and to be inwardly clean, no one being able to criticize you from now until our Lord returns.   Philippians 1:9,10 LB

**180.** Applying all diligence, in your faith supply moral excellence, and in your moral excellence, knowledge; and in your knowledge, self-control, and in your self-control, perseverance, and in your perseverance, godliness; and in your godliness, brotherly kindness, and in your brotherly kindness, Christian love. For if these qualities are yours and are increasing, they render you neither useless nor unfruitful in the true knowledge of our Lord Jesus Christ.   II Peter 1:5-8 NASB

# K. The Lord will baptize you in the Holy Spirit.

**KEY VERSE: 181.** *I baptize you in water for repentance; but he who is coming after me is mightier than I, and I am not even fit to remove his sandals; he himself will baptize you with the Holy Spirit and fire.   Matthew 3:11 NASB*

**182.** Blessed are they which do hunger and thirst after righteousness, for they shall be filled.   Matthew 5:6 KJV

**183.** I will put my Spirit within you so that you will obey my laws and do whatever I command.   Ezekiel 36:27 LB

**184.** I will ask the Father and he will give you another Comforter, and he will never leave you. He is the Holy Spirit, the Spirit who leads into all truth. The world at large cannot receive him, for it isn't looking for him and doesn't recognize him. But you do, for he lives with you now and some day shall be in you. John 14:16,17 LB

**185.** Do you not know that you are a temple of God, and that the Spirit of God dwells in you? I Corinthians 3:16 NASB

**186.** You shall receive power when the Holy Spirit has come upon you; and you shall be my witnesses both in Jerusalem, and in all Judea and Samaria, and even to the remotest part of the earth. Acts 1:8 NASB

**187.** Each one of you must turn from sin, return to God, and be baptized in the name of Jesus Christ for the forgiveness of your sins; then you also shall receive this gift, the Holy Spirit. Acts 2:38 LB

**188.** If even sinful persons like yourselves give children what they need, don't you realize that your heavenly Father will do at least as much, and give the Holy Spirit to those who ask for him? Luke 11:13 LB

**189.** For the promise is unto you, and to your children, and to all that are afar off, even as many as the Lord our God shall call. Acts 2:39 KJV

**190.** It shall come to pass afterward, that I will pour out my Spirit upon all flesh; and your sons and your daughters shall prophesy, your old men shall dream dreams, your young men shall see visions. Joel 2:28 KJV

**191.** But the helper, the Holy Spirit, whom the Father will send in my name, he will teach you all things, and bring to your remembrance all that I said to you. John 14:26 NASB

**192.** For by one Spirit are we all baptized into one body. I Corinthians 12:13 KJV

**193.** I will send you the Comforter—the Holy Spirit, the source of all truth. He will come to you from the Father and will tell you all about me. John 15:26 LB

**194.** Nevertheless I tell you the truth; It is expedient for you that I go away: for if I go not away, the Comforter will not come unto you; but if I depart, I will send him unto you.    John 16:7 KJV

**195.** Now we have received, not the spirit of the world, but the Spirit which is of God; that we might know the things that are freely given to us of God.    I Corinthians 2:12 KJV

**196.** That the blessing of Abraham might come on the Gentiles through Jesus Christ; that we might receive the promise of the Spirit through faith.    Galatians 3:14 KJV

**197.** Whoever drinks of the water that I shall give him shall never thirst; but the water that I shall give him shall become in him a well of water springing up to eternal life.    John 4:14 NASB

**198.** Behold, I will pour out my spirit unto you, I will make known my words unto you.    Proverbs 1:23 KJV

**199.** He has put his brand upon us—his mark of ownership—and given us his Holy Spirit in our hearts as guarantee that we belong to him, and as the first installment of all that he is going to give us.    II Corinthians 1:22 LB

**200.** In him, you also, after listening to the message of truth, the gospel of your salvation—having also believed, you were sealed in him with the Holy Spirit of promise.    Ephesians 1:13 NASB


# L. God will give you a new freedom.

**KEY VERSE: 201.** *If the Son sets you free, you will indeed be free.    John 8:36 LB*

**202.** You will know the truth, and the truth will set you free.    John 8:32 LB

**203.** When he, the Spirit of truth, is come, he will guide you into all truth.   John 16:13 KJV

**204.** For the power of the life-giving Spirit—and this power is mine through Christ Jesus—has freed me from the vicious circle of sin and death.   Romans 8:2 LB

**205.** Now the Lord is that Spirit: and where the Spirit of the Lord is, there is liberty.   II Corinthians 3:17 KJV

**206.** Thou shalt break the yoke of their burden and the staff on their shoulders, the rod of their oppressor.   Isaiah 9:4 NASB

**207.** Now you are free from the power of sin and are slaves of God, and his benefits to you include holiness and everlasting life.   Romans 6:22 LB

**208.** He keeps you from all evil, and preserves your life. He keeps his eye upon you as you come and go, and always guards you.   Psalm 121:7,8 LB

**209.** He has sent me to comfort the broken-hearted, to announce liberty to captives and to open the eyes of the blind.   Isaiah 61:1 LB

# M. God instills faith in you.

**KEY VERSE: 210.** *God has allotted to each a measure of faith.   Romans 12:3 NASB*

**211.** Because of his kindness you have been saved through trusting Christ. And even trusting is not of yourselves; it too is a gift from God.   Ephesians 2:8 LB

**212.** The fruit of the Spirit is love, joy, peace, longsuffering, gentleness, goodness, faith, meekness, temperance.   Galatians 5:22,23 KJV

**213.** And though you have not seen him, you love him, and though you do not see him now, but believe in him, you greatly rejoice with joy inexpressible and full of glory, obtaining as the outcome of your faith the salvation of your souls. I Peter 1:8,9 NASB

**214.** Now the just shall live by faith. Hebrews 10:38 KJV

**215.** You can never please God without faith, without depending on him. Anyone who wants to come to God must believe that there is a God and that he rewards those who sincerely look for him. Hebrews 11:6 LB

**216.** Knowing that the testing of your faith produces endurance. James 1:3 NASB

**217.** These trials are only to test your faith, to see whether or not it is strong and pure. It is being tested as fire tests gold and purifies it—and your faith is far more precious to God than mere gold; so if your faith remains strong after being tried in the test tube of fiery trials, it will bring you much praise and glory and honor on the day of his return. I Peter 1:7 LB

**218.** The man who finds life will find it through trusting God. Romans 1:17 LB

**219.** The Scripture has shut up all men under sin, that the promise by faith in Jesus Christ might be given to those who believe. Galatians 3:22 NASB

**220.** For now we are all children of God through faith in Jesus Christ. Galatians 3:26 LB

**221.** Unto you it is given to believe in him. Philippians 1:29 KJV

**222.** Whatever is born of God overcomes the world; and this is the victory that has overcome the world—our faith. I John 5:4 NASB

**223.** Faith comes from hearing, and hearing by the word of Christ. Romans 10:17 NASB

**224.** Be not slothful, but followers of them who through faith and patience inherit the promises. Hebrews 6:12 KJV

**225.** Anything is possible if you have faith. Mark 9:23 LB

**226.** Believe in the Lord your God, and you shall have success! Believe his prophets and everything will be all right! II Chronicles 20:20 LB

**227.** In every battle you will need faith as your shield to stop the fiery arrows aimed at you by Satan. Ephesians 6:16 LB

**228.** Believe on the Lord Jesus and you will be saved, and your entire household. Acts 16:31 LB

**229.** Blessed are they that have not seen, and yet have believed. John 20:29 KJV

**230.** For truly I say to you, if you have faith as a mustard seed, you shall say to this mountain "move from here to there," and it shall move; and nothing shall be impossible to you. Matthew 17:20 NASB

**231.** Truly if you have faith, and don't doubt, you can do things like this and much more. You can even say to this Mount of Olives "move over into the ocean," and it will. Matthew 21:21 LB

**232.** Truly I say to you, whoever says to this mountain, "Be taken up and cast into the sea" and does not doubt in his heart, but believes that what he says is going to happen; it shall be granted him. Mark 11:23 NASB

**233.** You can get anything—anything you ask for in prayer—if you believe. Matthew 21:22 LB

**234.** But if you stay in me and obey my commands, you may ask any request you like, and it will be granted! John 15:7 LB

**235.** You haven't tried this before, [but begin now]. Ask, using my name, and you will receive, and your cup of joy will overflow. John 16:24 LB

**236.** Whatsoever we ask, we receive of him, because we keep his commandments, and do those things that are pleasing in his sight. I John 3:22 KJV

**237.** This is the confidence which we have before him, that, if we ask anything according to his will, he hears us. And if we know that he hears us in whatever we ask, we know that we have the requests which we have asked from him. I John 5:14,15 NASB

**238.** Fight on for God. Hold tightly to the eternal life which God has given you, and which you have confessed with such a ringing confession before many witnesses. I Timothy 6:12 LB

**239.** You can ask him for anything, using my name, and I will do it, for this will bring praise to the Father because of what I, the Son, will do for you. John 14:13 LB

**240.** Yes, ask anything, using my name, and I will do it. John 14:14 LB

**241.** Therefore being justified by faith, we have peace with God through our Lord Jesus Christ. Romans 5:1 KJV

# N. Jesus Christ forgives your daily sins.

**KEY VERSE: 242.** *If any man sin, we have an advocate with the Father, Jesus Christ the righteous. I John 2:1 KJV*

**243.** Your sins are forgiven you for his name's sake. I John 2:12 KJV

**244.** If we confess our sins, he is faithful and just to forgive us our sins, and to cleanse us from all unrighteousness. I John 1:9 KJV

**245.** Sanctify them in the truth; thy word is truth. John 17:17 NASB

**246.** The very God of peace sanctify you wholly; and I pray God your whole spirit and soul and body be preserved blameless unto the coming of our Lord Jesus Christ. I Thessalonians 5:23 KJV

**247.** Although you were formerly alienated and hostile

in mind, engaged in evil deeds, yet he has now reconciled you in his fleshly body through death, in order to present you before him holy and blameless and beyond reproach.   Colossians 1:21,22 NASB

**248.** Your sins are washed away, and you are set apart for God, and he has accepted you because of what the Lord Jesus Christ and the Spirit of our God have done for you.   I Corinthians 6:11 LB

**249.** Who gave himself for us, that he might redeem us from all iniquity, and purify unto himself a peculiar people, zealous of good works.   Titus 2:14 KJV

**250.** I will also turn my hand against you, and will smelt away your dross as with lye, and will remove all your alloy.   Isaiah 1:25 NASB

**251.** Of him all the prophets bear witness that through his name every one who believes in him has received forgiveness of sins.   Acts 10:43 NASB

**252.** For God took the sinless Christ and poured into him our sins. Then, in exchange, he poured God's goodness into us.   II Corinthians 5:21 LB

**253.** And through him everyone who believes is freed from all things, from which you could not be freed through the law of Moses.   Acts 13:39 NASB

**254.** He has not punished us as we deserve for all our sins, for his mercy toward those who fear and honor him is as great as the height of the heavens above the earth.   Psalm 103:10,11 LB

# O. The Lord brings hope to you.

**KEY VERSE: 255.**   *O Lord, you alone are my hope; I've trusted you from childhood.   Psalm 71:5 LB*

**256.** For those who serve the Lord, he will redeem

them; everyone who takes refuge in him will be freely pardoned.   Psalm 34:22 LB

**257.** You will have courage because you will have hope.   Job 11:18 LB

**258.** Behold, the eye of the Lord is upon them that fear him, upon them that hope in his mercy to deliver their soul from death, and to keep them alive in famine.   Psalm 33:18,19 KJV

**259.** Everyone who has this hope fixed on him purifies himself, just as he is pure.   I John 3:3 NASB

**260.** The Lord shall help them, and deliver them: he shall deliver them from the wicked, and save them, because they trust in him.   Psalm 37:40 KJV

**261.** To whom God would make known what is the riches of the glory of this mystery among the Gentiles; which is Christ in you, the hope of glory.   Colossians 1:27 KJV

**262.** O my soul, don't be discouraged. Don't be upset. Expect God to act! For I know that I shall again have plenty of reason to praise him for all that he will do. He is my help! He is my God!   Psalm 42:11 LB

**263.** We may have strong encouragement, we who have fled for refuge in laying hold of the hope set before us. This hope we have as an anchor of the soul, a hope both sure and steadfast and one which enters within the veil.   Hebrews 6:18,19 NASB

**264.** Be strong, and let your heart take courage, all you who hope in the Lord.   Psalm 31:24 NASB

**265.** I know whom I have believed, and am persuaded that he is able to keep that which I have committed unto him against that day.   II Timothy 1:12 KJV

**266.** For this God is our God forever and ever: he will be our guide, even unto death.   Psalm 48:14 KJV

**267.** And hope does not disappoint; because the love of God has been poured out within our hearts through the Holy Spirit who was given to us.   Romans 5:5 NASB

**268.** For whatever was written in earlier times was written for our instruction, that through perseverance and the encouragement of the Scriptures we might have hope.   Romans 15:4 NASB

**269.** We rejoice in hope of the glory of God.   Romans 5:2 KJV


# P. The Word of God is alive.

**KEY VERSE: 270.** *Heaven and earth shall pass away, but my words shall not pass away.   Matthew 24:35 KJV*

**271.** The grass withers, the flowers fade, but the word of our God shall stand forever.   Isaiah 40:8 LB

**272.** The word of the Lord will last forever. And his message is the Good News that was preached to you.   I Peter 1:25 LB

**273.** All scripture is given by inspiration of God, and is profitable for doctrine, for reproof, for correction, for instruction in righteousness.   II Timothy 3:16 KJV

**274.** Thy word is a lamp unto my feet, and a light unto my path.   Psalm 119:105 KJV

**275.** I am not ashamed of the gospel of Christ: for it is the power of God unto salvation to every one that believeth.   Romans 1:16 KJV

**276.** The word of God is quick, and powerful, and sharper than any two-edged sword, piercing even to the dividing asunder of soul and spirit, and of the joints and marrow, and is a discerner of the thoughts and intents of the heart.   Hebrews 4:12 KJV

**277.** Take the helmet of salvation, and the sword of the Spirit, which is the word of God.   Ephesians 6:17 KJV

**278.** Man does not live by bread alone, but man lives by everything that proceeds out of the mouth of the Lord.   Deuteronomy 8:3 NASB

**279.** Like newborn babes, long for the pure milk of the word, that by it you may grow in respect to salvation, if you have tasted the kindness of the Lord.   I Peter 2:2,3 NASB

**280.** Be a good workman, one who does not need to be ashamed when God examines your work. Know what his word says and means.   II Timothy 2:15 LB

**281.** You search the Scriptures, for you believe they give you eternal life. And the Scriptures point to me!   John 5:39 LB

**282.** The law of the Lord is perfect, converting the soul; the testimony of the Lord is sure, making wise the simple. The statutes of the Lord are right, rejoicing the heart; the commandment of the Lord is pure, enlightening the eyes.   Psalm 19:7,8 KJV

**283.** The sacred writings which are able to give you the wisdom that leads to salvation through faith which is in Christ Jesus.   II Timothy 3:15 NASB

**284.** The commandment is a lamp; and the law is a light; and reproofs of instruction are the way of life.   Proverbs 6:23 KJV

**285.** Great peace have they which love thy law: and nothing shall offend them.   Psalm 119:165 KJV

**286.** All who fear God and trust in him are blessed beyond expression. Yes, happy is the man who delights in doing his commands.   Psalm 112:1 LB

**287.** So shall my word be which goes forth from my mouth; it shall not return to me empty, without accomplishing what I desire, and without succeeding in the matter for which I sent it.   Isaiah 55:11 NASB

**288.** So faith comes from hearing, and hearing by the word of Christ.   Romans 10:17 NASB

**289.** Blessed is he who reads and those who hear

the words of the prophecy, and heed the things which are written in it.   Revelation 1:3 NASB

## Q. God honors obedience.

**KEY VERSE: 290.** *Keep putting into practice all you learned from me and saw me doing, and the God of peace will be with you.   Philippians 4:9 LB*

**291.** Blessed are those who keep justice, who practice righteousness at all times.   Psalm 106:3 NASB

**292.** Has the Lord as much pleasure in your burnt offerings and sacrifices as in your obedience? Obedience is far better than sacrifice.   I Samuel 15:22 LB

**293.** If you will obey me and keep your part of my contract with you, you shall be my own little flock from among all the nations of the earth; for all the earth is mine.   Exodus 19:5 LB

**294.** If you keep my commandments, you will abide in my love; just as I have kept my Father's commandments, and abide in his love.   John 15:10 NASB

**295.** All who listen to my instructions and follow them are wise, like a man who builds his house on solid rock.   Matthew 7:24 LB

**296.** Jesus answered and said unto him, if a man love me, he will keep my words: and my Father will love him, and we will come unto him, and make our abode with him.   John 14:23 KJV

**297.** If anyone breaks the least commandment, and teaches others to, he shall be the least in the Kingdom of Heaven. But those who teach God's laws and obey them shall be great in the Kingdom of Heaven.   Matthew 5:19 LB

**298.** If any one serves me, let him follow me; and where I am, there shall my servant also be; if any one serves me, the Father will honor him.   John 12:26 NASB

**299.** Not all who sound religious are really godly people. They may refer to me as 'Lord,' but still won't get to heaven. For the decisive question is whether they obey my Father in heaven.   Matthew 7:21 LB

**300.** Whoever keeps doing the will of God will live forever.   I John 2:17 LB

**301.** You know these things—now do them! That is the path of blessing.   John 13:17 LB

**302.** If any man will do his will, he shall know of the doctrine, whether it be of God, or whether I speak of myself.   John 7:17 KJV

**303.** Whatsoever we ask, we receive of him, because we keep his commandments, and do those things that are pleasing in his sight.   I John 3:22 KJV

**304.** Obey the laws of God and follow all his ways; keep each of his commands written in the law of Moses so that you will prosper in everything you do, wherever you turn.   I Kings 2:3 LB

**305.** All the paths of the Lord are mercy and truth unto such as keep his covenant and his testimonies.   Psalm 25:10 KJV

**306.** If you consent and obey, you will eat the best of the land.   Isaiah 1:19 NASB

**307.** But what I told them was: Obey me and I will be your God and you shall be my people; only do as I say and all shall be well.   Jeremiah 7:23 LB

**308.** Now therefore, O sons, listen to me, for blessed are they who keep my ways.   Proverbs 8:32 NASB

**309.** Return to me, and I will return to you, says the Lord of hosts.   Malachi 3:7 NASB

**310.** If they obey and serve him, they shall spend their days in prosperity, and their years in pleasures.   Job 36:11 KJV

**311.** Blessed are they that keep his testimonies, and that seek him with the whole heart.   Psalm 119:2 KJV

**312.** Keep the commandments and keep your life; despising them means death.   Proverbs 19:16 LB

**313.** But one who looks intently at the perfect law, the law of liberty and abides by it, not having become a forgetful hearer but an effectual doer, this man shall be blessed in what he does.   James 1:25 NASB

**314.** He became the author of eternal salvation unto all them that obey him.   Hebrews 5:9 KJV

**315.** Blessed are they that do his commandments, that they may have right to the tree of life; and may enter in through the gates into the city.   Revelation 22:14 KJV

# R. God leaves surrender up to you.

**KEY VERSE: 316.** *Blessed are the poor in spirit: for theirs is the kingdom of heaven.   Matthew 5:3 KJV*

**317.** Take my yoke upon you, and learn from me, for I am gentle and humble in heart; and you shall find rest for your souls.   Matthew 11:29 NASB

**318.** Humble yourselves therefore under the mighty hand of God, that he may exalt you in due time.   I Peter 5:6 KJV

**319.** Blessed are they that hear the word of God, and keep it.   Luke 11:28 KJV

**320.** Submit yourselves for the Lord's sake to every human institution for such is the will of God that by doing right you may silence the ignorance of foolish men.   I Peter 2:13 NASB

**321.** You younger men, likewise, be subject to your elders; and all of you, clothe yourselves with humility toward one another, for God is opposed to the proud, but gives grace to the humble.   I Peter 5:5 NASB

**322.** Whosoever therefore shall humble himself as this

little child, the same is greatest in the kingdom of heaven.   Matthew 18:4 KJV

**323.** Submit yourselves therefore to God. Resist the devil, and he will flee from you.   James 4:7 KJV

**324.** Humble yourselves in the sight of the Lord, and he shall lift you up.   James 4:10 NASB

**325.** It is good that a man should both hope and quietly wait for the salvation of the Lord.   Lamentations 3:26 KJV

**326.** By humility and the fear of the Lord are riches, and honor, and life.   Proverbs 22:4 KJV

**327.** Jesus replied, I am the Bread of Life. No one coming to me will ever be hungry again.   John 6:35 LB

**328.** All that the Father gives me shall come to me; and the one who comes to me I will certainly not cast out.   John 6:37 NASB

# S. God honors holiness.

**KEY VERSE: 329.** *Godliness is profitable unto all things, having promise of the life that now is, and of that which is to come.   I Timothy 4:8 KJV*

**330.** Don't copy the behavior and customs of this world, but be a new and different person with a fresh newness in all you do and think. Then you will learn from your own experience how his ways will really satisfy you.   Romans 12:2 LB

**331.** If you do this you will experience God's peace, which is far more wonderful than the human mind can understand. His peace will keep your thoughts and your hearts quiet and at rest as you trust in Christ Jesus.   Philippians 4:7 LB

**332.** Draw near to God and he will draw near to you.

Cleanse your hands, you sinners; and purify your hearts, you double-minded.   James 4:8 NASB

**333.** Righteousness shall go before him; and shall set us in the way of his steps. Psalm 85:13 KJV

**334.** The man who tries to be good, loving and kind finds life, righteousness and honor.   Proverbs 21:21 LB

**335.** Yet the Lord pleads with you still: Ask where the good road is, the godly paths you used to walk in, in the days of long ago. Travel there, and you will find rest for your souls.   Jeremiah 6:16 LB

**336.** He who sows righteousness gets a true reward.   Proverbs 11:18 NASB

**337.** You bless the godly man, O Lord; you protect him with your shield of love.   Psalm 5:12 LB

**338.** A highway will be there, a roadway, and it will be called the highway of holiness.   Isaiah 35:8 NASB

**339.** I have come as a light to shine in this dark world, so that all who put their trust in me will no longer wander in the darkness.   John 12:46 LB

**340.** O Lord, who may abide in thy tent? Who may dwell on thy holy hill? He who walks with integrity, and works righteousness, and speaks truth in his heart. Psalm 15:1,2 NASB

**341.** For the Lord is righteous; he loves righteousness; the upright will behold his face.   Psalm 11:7 NASB

**342.** For the eyes of the Lord move to and fro throughout the earth that he may strongly support those whose heart is completely his.   II Chronicles 16:9 NASB

**343.** If our heart condemn us not, then have we confidence toward God.   I John 3:21 KJV

**344.** The Lord observes the good deeds done by godly men, and gives them eternal rewards.   Psalm 37:18 LB

**345.** For the mind set on the flesh is death, but the mind set on the Spirit is life and peace.   Romans 8:6 NASB

**346.** Blessed are the undefiled in the way, who walk in the law of the Lord.   Psalm 119:1 KJV

**347.** Such as are upright in their way are his delight.   Proverbs 11:20 KJV

**348.** He stores up sound wisdom for the upright; he is a shield to those who walk in integrity.   Proverbs 2:7 NASB

**349.** Them that honor me I will honor.   I Samuel 2:30 KJV

# T. God blesses clean conversation.

**KEY VERSE: 350.** *Those who walk my paths will receive salvation from the Lord.   Psalm 50:23 LB*

**351.** Do you want a long, good life. Then watch your tongue! Keep your lips from lying.   Psalm 34:12,13 LB

**352.** A wholesome tongue is a tree of life.   Proverbs 15:4 KJV

**353.** Everyone enjoys giving good advice, and how wonderful it is to be able to say the right thing at the right time.   Proverbs 15:23 LB

**354.** Your words now reflect your fate then: either you will be justified by them or you will be condemned.   Matthew 12:37 LB

**355.** If you confess with your mouth Jesus as Lord, and believe in your heart that God raised him from the dead, you shall be saved; for with the heart man believes, resulting in righteousness, and with the mouth he confesses, resulting in salvation.   Romans 10:9,10 NASB

**356.** Pleasant words are as an honeycomb, sweet to the soul, and health to the bones.   Proverbs 16:24 KJV

**357.** He who guards his mouth and his tongue guards his soul from troubles.   Proverbs 21:23 NASB

**358.** He who has clean hands and a pure heart, who

has not lifted up his soul to falsehood, and has not sworn deceitfully, he shall receive a blessing from the Lord and righteousness from the God of his salvation. Psalm 24:4,5 NASB

**359.** Whoever confesses that Jesus is the Son of God, God abides in him, and he in God. I John 4:15 NASB

**360.** Every one therefore who shall confess me before men, I will also confess him before my Father who is in heaven. Matthew 10:32 NASB

**361.** From a wise mind comes careful and persuasive speech. Proverbs 16:23 LB

**362.** The mouth of the righteous flows with wisdom. Proverbs 10:31 NASB

**363.** The lips of the righteous know what is acceptable. Proverbs 10:32 KJV

**364.** For I will give you the right words and such logic that none of your opponents will be able to reply! Luke 21:15 LB

**365.** To one is given by the Spirit the word of wisdom; to another the word of knowledge by the same Spirit. I Corinthians 12:8 KJV

**366.** The preparations of the heart in man, and the answer of the tongue, is from the Lord. Proverbs 16:1 KJV

**367.** Let your way of life be free from the love of money, being content with what you have; for he himself has said, ''I will never desert you, nor will I ever forsake you.'' Hebrews 13:5 NASB

**368.** He that will love life, and see good days, let him refrain his tongue from evil, and his lips that they speak no guile. I Peter 3:10 KJV

**369.** The lip of truth shall be established forever; but a lying tongue is but for a moment. Proverbs 12:19 KJV

**370.** O Lord, who may abide in thy tent? Who may dwell on thy holy hill? He who walks with integrity, and works righteousness, and speaks truth in his heart. He does not slander with his tongue, nor does evil to his neighbor, nor takes up a reproach against his friend.   Psalm 15:1,2,3 NASB

**371.** A soft answer turns away wrath, but harsh words cause quarrels.   Proverbs 15:1 LB


## U. God will bless your family.

**KEY VERSE: 372.** *I will give them one heart, and one way, that they may fear me forever, for the good of them, and of their children after them.   Jeremiah 32:39 KJV*

**373.** The Lord shall increase you more and more, you and your children.   Psalm 115:14 KJV

**374.** You must obey these laws that I will tell you today, so that all will be well with you and your children.   Deuteronomy 4:40 LB

**375.** A righteous man who walks in his integrity—how blessed are his sons after him.   Proverbs 20:7 NASB

**376.** In the fear of the Lord is strong confidence; and his children shall have a place of refuge.   Proverbs 14:26 KJV

**377.** You shall rejoice in all the good which the Lord your God has given you and your household.   Deuteronomy 26:11 NASB

**378.** Children are a heritage of the Lord.   Psalm 127:3 KJV

**379.** The father of the righteous will greatly rejoice, and he who begets a wise son will be glad in him.   Proverbs 23:24 NASB

**380.** Children, obey your parents in all things; for this is well pleasing unto the Lord.   Colossians 3:20 KJV

**381.** Honor your father and mother. This is the first

of God's ten commandments that ends with a promise. And this is the promise: that if you honor your father and mother, yours will be a long life, full of blessing. Ephesians 6:2,3 LB

**382.** Train up a child in the way he should go; and when he is old, he will not depart from it. Proverbs 22:6 KJV

# V. God prospers the charitable.

**KEY VERSE: 383.** *When you did it to these my brothers you were doing it to me! Matthew 25:40 LB*

**384.** If anyone so much as gives you a cup of water because you are Christ's—I say this solemnly—he won't lose his reward. Mark 9:41

**385.** If you give to the poor, your needs will be supplied! Proverbs 28:27 LB

**386.** If you give yourself to the hungry, and satisfy the desire of the afflicted, then your light will rise in darkness, and your gloom will become like midday. Isaiah 58:10 NASB

**387.** Bring all the tithes into the storehouse so that there will be food enough in my temple; if you do, I will open up the windows of heaven for you and pour out a blessing so great you won't have room enough to take it in! Malachi 3:10 LB

**388.** The generous man will be prosperous, and he who waters will himself be watered. Proverbs 11:25 NASB

**389.** If you give little, you will get little. A farmer who plants just a few seeds will get only a small crop, but if he plants much, he will reap much. II Corinthians 9:6 LB

**390.** Blessed are the merciful: for they shall obtain mercy.   Matthew 5:7 KJV

**391.** Every one must make up his own mind as to how much he should give. Don't force anyone to give more than he really wants to, for cheerful givers are the ones God prizes.   II Corinthians 9:7 LB

**392.** Be strong and do not lose courage, for there is reward for your work.   II Chronicles 15:7 NASB

**393.** God blesses those who are kind to the poor. He helps them out of their troubles.   Psalm 41:1 LB

**394.** God is able to make all grace abound to you, that always having all sufficiency in everything, you may have an abundance for every good deed.   II Corinthians 9:8 NASB

**395.** When you help the poor you are lending to the Lord—and he pays wonderful interest on your loan. Proverbs 19:17 LB

**396.** If you give, you will get! Your gift will return to you in full and overflowing measure, pressed down, shaken together to make room for more, and running over. Whatever measure you use to give—large or small—will be used to measure what is given back to you.   Luke 6:38 LB

# W. God wants us to live in peace and unity.

**KEY VERSE: 397.** *Be perfect, be of good comfort, be of one mind, live in peace; and the God of love and peace shall be with you.   II Corinthians 13:11 KJV*

**398.** By this all men will know that you are my disciples, if you have love for one another.   John 13:35 NASB

**399.** Behold, how good and pleasant it is for brethren

to dwell together in unity.   Psalm 133:1 KJV

**400.** The one who loves his brother abides in the light and there is no cause for stumbling in him.   I John 2:10 NASB

**401.** Blessed are the peacemakers; for they shall be called the children of God.   Matthew 5:9 KJV

**402.** We know that we have passed from death unto life, because we love the brethren.   I John 3:14 KJV

**403.** To the counselors of peace is joy.   Proverbs 12:20 KJV

**404.** For though we have never yet seen God, when we love each other God lives in us and his love within us grows ever stronger.   I John 4:12 LB

**405.** If your enemy is hungry, give him food. If he is thirsty, give him something to drink. This will make him feel ashamed of himself, and God will reward you.   Proverbs 25:21,22 LB

**406.** My little children, let us not love in word, neither in tongue; but in deed and in truth. And hereby we know that we are of the truth, and shall assure our hearts before him.   I John 3:18,19 KJV

**407.** Not returning evil for evil, or insult for insult, but giving a blessing instead; for you were called for the very purpose that you might inherit a blessing.   I Peter 3:9 NASB

**408.** Love your enemies! Do good to them! Lend to them! And don't be concerned about the fact that they won't repay. Then your reward from heaven will be very great, and you will truly be acting as sons of God.   Luke 6:35 LB

# X. God calls us to witness for Him.

**KEY VERSE: 409.** *Follow me, and I will make you fishers of men.   Matthew 4:19 KJV*

**410.** Godly men are growing a tree that bears life—giving fruit, and all who win souls are wise.   Proverbs 11:30 LB

**411.** And those who are wise—the people of God—shall shine as brightly as the sun's brilliance, and those who turn many to righteousness will glitter like stars forever.   Daniel 12:3 LB

**412.** Don't be afraid! Speak out! Don't quit! For I am with you and no one can harm you.   Acts 18:9,10 LB

**413.** You shall receive power when the Holy Spirit has come upon you; and you shall be my witnesses both in Jerusalem, and in all Judea and Samaria, and even to the remotest part of the earth.   Acts 1:8 NASB

**414.** The Holy Spirit will give you the right words even as you are standing there.   Luke 12:12 LB

**415.** The Comforter, which is the Holy Ghost, whom the Father will send in my name, he shall teach you all things, and bring all things to your remembrance, whatsoever I have said unto you.   John 14:26 KJV

**416.** I have put my words in your mouth, and have covered you with the shadow of my hand.   Isaiah 51:16 NASB

**417.** It will lead to an opportunity for your testimony.   Luke 21:13 NASB

**418.** For I will give you utterance and wisdom which none of your opponents will be able to resist or refute.   Luke 21:15 NASB

**419.** Now go ahead and do as I tell you, for I will help you to speak well, and I will tell you what to say.   Exodus 4:12 LB

**420.** The Lord God has given me his words of wisdom so that I may know what I should say to all these weary ones.   Isaiah 50:4 LB

**421.** Therefore, thus says the Lord, the God of hosts, "Because you have spoken this word, behold, I am making my words in your mouth fire."   Jeremiah 5:14 NASB

**422.** Let your light so shine before men, that they may see your good works and glorify your Father which is in heaven.   Matthew 5:16 KJV

**423.** Let him know that he who turns a sinner from the error of his way will save his soul from death, and will cover a multitude of sins.   James 5:20 NASB

**424.** There will be glory and honor and peace from God for all who obey him, whether they are Jews or Gentiles.   Romans 2:10 LB

**425.** Pay close attention to yourself and to your teaching; persevere in these things; for as you do this you will insure salvation both for yourself and for those who hear you.   I Timothy 4:16 NASB

**426.** For God is not unfair. How can he forget your hard work for him, or forget the way you used to show your love for him—and still do—by helping his children?   Hebrews 6:10 LB

**427.** Already he who reaps is receiving wages, and is gathering fruit for life eternal; that he who sows and he who reaps may rejoice together.   John 4:36 NASB

**428.** Therefore, my beloved brethren, be steadfast, immovable, always abounding in the work of the Lord, knowing that your toil is not in vain in the Lord.   I Corinthians 15:58 NASB

**429.** And let us not be weary in well doing: for in due season we shall reap, if we faint not.   Galatians 6:9 KJV

*Whatever is good*

*and perfect comes to us*

*from God, the Creator of all light,*

*and he shines forever*

*without change or shadow.*

*James 1:17 LB*

# GOD'S PROMISES
# FOR YOUR
# PERSONAL NEEDS

## A. Do you have doubts and fears?

**KEY VERSE: 430.** *For I can do everything God asks me to with the help of Christ who gives me the strength and power.* *Philippians 4:13 LB*

**431.** Not that we are sufficient of ourselves to think anything as of ourselves; but our sufficiency is of God.   II Corinthians 3:5 KJV

**432.** Being fully persuaded that what he had promised, he was able also to perform.   Romans 4:21 KJV

**433.** He is faithful that promised.   Hebrews 10:23 KJV

**434.** Fear not, for I am with you. Do not be dismayed. I am your God. I will strengthen you; I will help you; I will uphold you with my victorious right hand.   Isaiah 41:10 LB

**435.** My covenant will I not break, nor alter the thing that is gone out of my lips.   Psalm 89:34 KJV

**436.** I have spoken it, I will also bring it to pass; I have purposed it, I will also do it.   Isaiah 46:11 KJV

**437.** For I am the Lord, I change not.   Malachi 3:6 KJV

**438.** They shall call on my name, and I will hear them: I will say, It is my people; and they shall say, The Lord is my God.   Zechariah 13:9 KJV

**439.** Ask, and you will be given what you ask for. Seek, and you will find. Knock, and the door will be opened.

For everyone who asks, receives. Anyone who seeks, finds. If only you will knock, the door will open.   Matthew 7:7,8 LB

**440.** The effective prayer of a righteous man can accomplish much.   James 5:16 NASB

**441.** Faithful is he who calls you, and he also will bring it to pass.   I Thessalonians 5:24 NASB

**442.** The sum of thy word is truth, and every one of thy righteous ordinances is everlasting.   Psalm 119:160 NASB

**443.** He shall not be afraid of evil tidings: his heart is fixed, trusting in the Lord.   Psalm 112:7 KJV

**444.** The Lord is not slow about his promise, as some count slowness, but is patient toward you, not wishing for any to perish but for all to come to repentance.   II Peter 3:9 NASB

**445.** He carries out and fulfills all of God's promises, no matter how many of them there are; and we have told everyone how faithful he is, giving glory to his name.   II Corinthians 1:20 LB

**446.** For the Lord God is a sun and shield: the Lord will give grace and glory; no good thing will he withhold from them that walk uprightly.   Psalm 84:11 KJV

**447.** You will pray to him, and he will hear you.   Job 22:27 NASB

**448.** How true it is, and how I long that everyone should know it, that Christ Jesus came into the world to save sinners.   I Timothy 1:15 LB

**449.** Then you will call, and the Lord will answer; you will cry, and he will say, 'Here I am.'   Isaiah 58:9 NASB

**450.** Yes, the Lord hears the good man when he calls to him for help, and saves him out of all his troubles.   Psalm 34:17 LB

**451.** In whom we have boldness and access with confidence by the faith of him.   Ephesians 3:12 KJV

**452.** But know that the Lord hath set apart him that

is godly for himself: the Lord will hear when I call unto him.   Psalm 4:3 KJV

**453.** The eyes of the Lord are upon the righteous, and his ears are open to their cry.   Psalm 34:15 KJV

**454.** Do not seek what you shall eat, and what you shall drink, and do not keep worrying. But seek for his kingdom, and these things shall be added to you.   Luke 12:29,31 NASB

# B. Is it hard to keep your life clean?

**KEY VERSE: 455.** *Your sins are washed away, and you are set apart for God, and he has accepted you because of what the Lord Jesus Christ and the Spirit of our God have done for you.   I Corinthians 6:11 LB*

**456.** Unto him that is able to keep you from falling, and to present you faultless before the presence of his glory with exceeding joy.   Jude 24 KJV

**457.** If any man be in Christ, he is a new creature: old things are passed away; behold, all things are become new.   II Corinthians 5:17 KJV

**458.** You are already clean because of the word which I have spoken to you.   John 15:3 NASB

**459.** Come, let's talk this over! says the Lord; no matter how deep the stain of your sins, I can take it out and make you as clean as freshly fallen snow. Even if you are stained as red as crimson, I can make you white as wool.   Isaiah 1:18 LB

**460.** Not by works of righteousness which we have done, but according to his mercy he saved us, by the washing of regeneration, and renewing of the Holy Ghost; which he shed on us abundantly through Jesus Christ our Saviour.   Titus 3:5,6 KJV

**461.** Iniquities prevail against me: as for our transgressions, thou shalt purge them away. Psalm 65:3 KJV

**462.** Christ also loved the church, and gave himself for it; that he might sanctify and cleanse it with the washing of water by the word. Ephesians 5:25 KJV

**463.** If we walk in the light as he himself is in the light, we have fellowship with one another, and the blood of Jesus his Son cleanses us from all sin. I John 1:7 NASB

**464.** Just think how much more surely the blood of Christ will transform our lives and hearts. His sacrifice frees us from the worry of having to obey the old rules, and makes us want to serve the living God. Hebrews 9:14 LB

**465.** The Lord has rewarded me according to my righteousness; according to the cleanness of my hands he has recompensed me. II Samuel 22:21 NASB

**466.** And an highway shall be there, and a way, and it shall be called, The way of holiness; the unclean shall not pass over it. Isaiah 35:8 KJV

**467.** Let us draw near with a true heart, in full assurance of faith, having our hearts sprinkled from an evil conscience, and our bodies washed with pure water. Hebrews 10:22 KJV

**468.** Commit your work to the Lord, then it will succeed. Proverbs 16:3 LB

**469.** Let the wicked forsake his way, and the unrighteous man his thoughts: and let him return unto the Lord, and he will have mercy upon him; and to our God, for he will abundantly pardon. Isaiah 55:7 KJV

**470.** I pray God your whole spirit and soul and body be preserved blameless unto the coming of our Lord Jesus Christ. I Thessalonians 5:23 KJV

**471.** Blessed are the pure in heart for they shall see God. Matthew 5:8 KJV

# C. Do you need peace of mind?

**KEY VERSE: 472.** *You will experience God's peace, which is far more wonderful than the human mind can understand. His peace will keep your thoughts and your hearts quiet and at rest as you trust in Christ Jesus. Philippians 4:7 LB*

**473.** The work of righteousness shall be peace; and the effect of righteousness, quietness and assurance forever.   Isaiah 32:17 KJV

**474.** He will speak peace unto his people, and to his saints.   Psalm 85:8 KJV

**475.** Peace I leave with you; my peace I give to you; not as the world gives, do I give to you.   John 14:27 NASB

**476.** Come to me, all who are weary and heavy laden, and I will give you rest.   Matthew 11:28 NASB

**477.** The Lord will give strength unto his people: the Lord will bless his people with peace.   Psalm 29:11 KJV

**478.** For God has not given us a spirit of timidity, but of power and love and discipline.   II Timothy 1:7 NASB

**479.** Great peace have they which love thy law: and nothing shall offend them.   Psalm 119:165 KJV

**480.** He will keep in perfect peace all those who trust in him, whose thoughts turn often to the Lord.   Isaiah 26:3 LB

**481.** Surely goodness and mercy shall follow me all the days of my life: and I will dwell in the house of the Lord forever.   Psalm 23:6 KJV

**482.** You will have courage because you will have hope. You will take your time, and rest in safety. You will lie down unafraid and many will look to you for help.   Job 11:18,19 LB

**483.** He will shield you with his wings! They will shelter you. His faithful promises are your armor.   Psalm 91:4 LB

**484.** No evil will befall you, nor will any plague come near your tent. Psalm 91:10 NASB

**485.** Don't be afraid, for I am with you. Isaiah 43:5 LB

**486.** When you lie down, you will not be afraid; when you lie down, your sleep will be sweet. Proverbs 3:24 NASB

**487.** Godliness with contentment is great gain. I Timothy 6:6 KJV

**488.** Your faith has saved you; go in peace. Luke 7:50 LB

**489.** Now may the Lord of peace himself continually grant you peace in every circumstance. II Thessalonians 3:16 NASB

**490.** Stay away from the love of money; be satisfied with what you have. For God has said "I will never, never fail you nor forsake you." Hebrews 13:5 LB

# D. Are you often tempted?

KEY VERSE: **491.** *In all these things we are more than conquerors, through him that loved us. Romans 8:37 KJV*

**492.** God is faithful, who will not allow you to be tempted beyond what you are able; but with the temptation will provide the way of escape also, that you may be able to endure it. I Corinthians 10:13 NASB

**493.** The Lord can rescue you and me from the temptations that surround us. II Peter 2:9 LB

**494.** For since he himself was tempted in that which he has suffered, he is able to come to the aid of those who are tempted. Hebrews 2:18 NASB

**495.** I am with you; that is all you need. My power

shows up best in weak people.   II Corinthians 12:9 LB

**496.** I have prayed for you, that your faith may not fail.   Luke 22:32 NASB

**497.** I'm not asking you to take them out of the world, but to keep them safe from Satan's power.   John 17:15 LB

**498.** Be of good cheer; I have overcome the world. John 16:33 KJV

**499.** Whatever is born of God overcomes the world; and this is the victory that has overcome the world—our faith.   I John 5:4 NASB

**500.** Resist the devil, and he will flee from you.   James 4:7 KJV

**501.** The God of peace will soon crush Satan under your feet.   Romans 16:20 LB

**502.** For it is he who delivers you from the snare of the trapper, and from the deadly pestilence.   Psalm 91:3 NASB

**503.** Be not overcome of evil, but overcome evil with good.   Romans 12:21 KJV

**504.** Let us hold fast the profession of our faith without wavering; (for he is faithful that promised).   Hebrews 10:23 KJV

**505.** Walk steadily forward to God without fear.   Job 11:15 LB

**506.** Since future victory is sure, be strong and steady, always abounding in the Lord's work, for you know that nothing you do for the Lord is ever wasted.   I Corinthians 15:58 LB

**507.** Who gave himself for our sins, that he might deliver us from this present evil world.   Galatians 1:4 KJV

**508.** He that overcometh shall inherit all things; and I will be his God, and he shall be my son.   Revelation 21:7 KJV

**509.** To him that overcometh will I grant to sit with

me in my throne, even as I also overcame, and am set down with my Father in his throne.   Revelation 3:21 KJV

**510.** Happy is the man who doesn't give in and do wrong when he is tempted, for afterwards he will get as his reward the crown of life that God has promised those who love him.   James 1:12 LB

**511.** You are from God, little children, and have overcome them; because greater is he who is in you than he who is in the world.   I John 4:4 NASB

# E. Are you hung-up with guilt?

**KEY VERSE: 512.** *There is therefore now no condemnation for those who are in Christ Jesus.   Romans 8:1 NASB*

**513.** Yet now God declares us "not guilty" of offending him if we trust in Jesus Christ, who in his kindness freely takes away our sins.   Romans 3:24 LB

**514.** For God took the sinless Christ and poured into him our sins. Then, in exchange, he poured God's goodness into us.   II Corinthians 5:21 LB

**515.** And having chosen us, he called us to come to him; and when we came, he declared us "not guilty," filled us with Christ's goodness, gave us right standing with himself, and promised us his glory.   Romans 8:30 LB

**516.** Everyone who trusts in him is freed from all guilt and declared righteous—something the Jewish law could never do.   Acts 13:39 LB

**517.** Being justified by faith, we have peace with God through our Lord Jesus Christ.   Romans 5:1 KJV

**518.** And because of what he has experienced, my righteous Servant shall make many to be counted righteous before God, for he shall bear all their sins.    Isaiah 53:11 LB

**519.** Who dares accuse us whom God has chosen for his own? Will God? No! He is the one who has forgiven us and given us right standing with himself.    Romans 8:33 LB

**520.** Who then will condemn us? Will Christ? No! For he is the one who died for us and came back to life again for us and is sitting at the place of highest honor next to God, pleading for us there in heaven.    Romans 8:34 LB

**521.** Being now justified by his blood, we shall be saved from wrath through him.    Romans 5:9 KJV

**522.** Christ's righteousness makes men right with God, so that they can live.    Romans 5:18 LB

**523.** I, even I, am the one who wipes out your transgressions for my own sake; and I will not remember your sins.    Isaiah 43:25 NASB

**524.** As far as the east is from the west, so far has he removed our transgressions from us.    Psalm 103:12 NASB

**525.** I've blotted out your sins; they are gone like morning mist at noon! Oh, return to me, for I have paid the price to set you free.    Isaiah 44:22 LB

**526.** Their sins and iniquities will I remember no more.    Hebrews 10:17 KJV

**527.** He will again have compassion on us; he will tread our iniquities underfoot. Yes, thou wilt cast all their sins into the depths of the sea.    Micah 7:19 NASB

**528.** I will forgive their iniquity, and I will remember their sin no more.    Jeremiah 31:34 KJV

**529.** I will be merciful to their unrighteousness, and their sins and their iniquities will I remember no more.    Hebrews 8:12 KJV

**530.** He forgives all my sins. He heals me.    Psalm 103:3 LB

**531.** So overflowing is his kindness toward us that he took away all our sins through the blood of his Son, by whom we are saved.  Ephesians 1:7 LB

**532.** No matter how deep the stain of your sins, I can take it out and make you as clean as freshly fallen snow. Even if you are stained as red as crimson, I can make you white as wool!  Isaiah 1:18 LB

**533.** I will cleanse them from all their iniquity, whereby they have sinned against me; and I will pardon all their iniquities, whereby they have sinned, and whereby they have transgressed against me.  Jeremiah 33:8 KJV

**534.** If any man sin, we have an advocate with the Father, Jesus Christ the righteous.  I John 2:1 KJV

**535.** He was wounded for our transgressions, he was bruised for our iniquities: the chastisement of our peace was upon him; and with his stripes we are healed. Isaiah 53:5 KJV

**536.** The blood of Jesus in his Son cleanses us from every sin.  I John 1:7 LB

**537.** How much more shall the blood of Christ, who through the eternal Spirit offered himself without spot to God, purge your conscience from dead works to serve the living God.  Hebrews 9:14 KJV

**538.** Any sin and blasphemy shall be forgiven men, but blasphemy against the Spirit shall not be forgiven. And whoever shall speak a word against the Son of Man, it shall be forgiven him.  Matthew 12:31,32 NASB

**539.** Blessed is he whose transgression is forgiven, whose sin is covered.  Psalm 32:1 KJV

**540.** What happiness for those whose guilt has been forgiven! What joys when sins are covered over! What relief for those who have confessed their sins and God has cleared their record.  Psalm 32:1,2 LB

**541.** All of us like sheep have gone astray, each of us has turned to his own way; but the Lord has caused the iniquity of us all to fall on him.  Isaiah 53:6 NASB

**542.** If we confess our sins, he is faithful and just to

**542.** If we confess our sins, he is faithful and just to forgive us our sins, and to cleanse us from all unrighteousness.   I John 1:9   KJV


# F. Does your life lack direction?

**KEY VERSE: 543.** *In everything you do, put God first,
and he will direct you and crown your efforts with success.   Proverbs 3:6 LB*

**544.** The steps of good men are directed by the Lord.
He delights in each step they take.   Psalm 37:23 LB

**545.** I will lead them in paths that they have not known.
I will make darkness light before them, and crooked things
straight. These things will I do unto them, and not forsake
them.   Isaiah 42:16 KJV

**546.** I will instruct you and teach you in the way which
you should go. I will counsel you with my eye upon
you.   Psalm 32:8 NASB

**547.** If you leave God's paths and go astray, you will
hear a Voice behind you say, "No, this is the way; walk
here."   Isaiah 30:21 LB

**548.** Commit you way to the Lord, trust also in him and
he will do it.   Psalm 37:5 NASB

**549.** To give light to them that sit in darkness and in the
shadow of death, to guide our feet into the way of peace.
Luke 1:79 KJV

**550.** The meek will he guide in judgment: and the meek
will he teach his way.   Psalm 25:9 KJV

**551.** For this God is our God for ever and ever: he will
be our guide even unto death.   Psalm 48:14 KJV

**552.** You will keep on guiding me all my life with your
wisdom and counsel; and afterwards receive me into the
glories of heaven!   Psalm 73:24 LB

**553.** Man's goings are of the Lord; how can a man

then understand his own way?   Proverbs 20:24 KJV

**554.** If I take the wings of the dawn, if I dwell in the remotest part of the sea, even there thy hand will lead me, and thy right hand will lay hold of me.   Psalm 139:9,10 NASB

**555.** He guides me in the paths of righteousness for his name's sake.   Psalm 23:3 NASB

**556.** For the Lord in his mercy will lead them beside the cool waters.   Isaiah 49:10 LB

**557.** He makes me lie down in green pastures; he leads me beside quiet waters.   Psalm 23:2 NASB

**558.** Howbeit, when he, the Spirit of truth, is come, he will guide you into all truth.   John 16:13 KJV

**559.** Thy word is a lamp unto my feet, and a light unto my path.   Psalm 119:105 KJV

**560.** I will direct their work in truth.   Isaiah 61:8 KJV

**561.** We should make plans—counting on God to direct us.   Proverbs 16:9 LB

**562.** The Lord will continually guide you.   Isaiah 58:11 NASB


# G. Are finances always a worry?

**KEY VERSE: 563.** *My God shall supply all your need according to his riches in glory by Christ Jesus.   Philippians 4:19 KJV*

**564.** Keep on asking and you will keep on getting; keep on looking and you will keep on finding; knock and the door will be opened.   Luke 11:9 LB

**565.** Consider the ravens, for they neither sow nor reap; and they have no storeroom nor barn; and yet God feeds them; how much more valuable you are than the birds!   Luke 12:24 NASB

**566.** Let him have all your worries and cares, for he

is always thinking about you and watching everything that concerns you.  I Peter 5:7 LB

**567.** The Lord will give grace and glory; no good thing will he withhold from them that walk uprightly.  **Psalm 84:11 KJV**

**568.** Your heavenly Father knows that you need all these things.  **Matthew 6:32 NASB**

**569.** Until now you have asked for nothing in my name; ask, and you will receive, that your joy may be made full.  **John 16:24 NASB**

**570.** Fear not, little flock; for it is your Father's good pleasure to give you the kingdom.  **Luke 12:32 KJV**

**571.** Trust in the Lord instead. Be kind and good to others; then you will live safely here in the land and prosper, feeding in safety.  **Psalm 37:3 LB**

**572.** I have been young, and now am old; yet have I not seen the righteous forsaken, nor his seed begging bread.  **Psalm 37:25 KJV**

**573.** If you hardhearted, sinful men know how to give good gifts to your children, won't your Father in heaven even more certainly give good gifts to those who ask him for them?  **Matthew 7:11 LB**

**574.** But seek for his kingdom, and these things shall be added to you.  **Luke 12:31 NASB**

**575.** It is better to have little and be godly than to own an evil man's wealth.  **Psalm 37:16 LB**

**576.** Indeed the very hairs of your head are all numbered. Do not fear; you are of more value than many sparrows.  **Luke 12:7 NASB**

**577.** If then God so clothes the grass, which is today in the field, and tomorrow is cast into the oven; how much more will he clothe you?  **Luke 12:28 KJV**

**578.** Your Father knows that you need these things.  **Luke 12:30 NASB**

**579.** The Lord has been mindful of us; he will bless us.  **Psalm 115:12 NASB**

**580.** Therefore, obey the terms of this covenant so that you will prosper in everything you do.   Deuteronomy 29:9 LB

**581.** They are like trees along a river bank bearing luscious fruit each season without fail. Their leaves shall never wither, and all they do shall prosper.   Psalm 1:3 LB

**582.** Then you shall prosper, if you are careful to observe the statutes and the ordinances which the Lord commanded Moses concerning Israel. Be strong and courageous, do not fear nor be dismayed.   I Chronicles 22:13 NASB

**583.** As long as he sought the Lord, God made him to prosper.   II Chronicles 26:5 KJV

**584.** Therefore I say to you, all things for which you pray and ask, believe that you have received them, and they shall be granted you.   Mark 11:24 NASB

**585.** You can ask him for anything, using my name, and I will do it, for this will bring praise to the Father because of what I, the Son, will do for you.   John 14:13 LB

**586.** Yes, ask anything, using my name, and I will do it.   John 14:14 LB


# H. Are you unhappy?

**KEY VERSE: 587.** *They that sow in tears shall reap in joy.   Psalm 126:5 KJV*

**588.** Yes, they go out weeping, carrying seed for sowing, and return singing, carrying their sheaves. Psalm 126:6 LB

**589.** The joy of the Lord is your strength.   Nehemiah 8:10 KJV

**590.** Our heart shall rejoice in him, because we have

trusted in his holy name.   Psalm 33:21 KJV

**591.** I will rejoice in the Lord, I will joy in the God of my salvation.   Habakkuk 3:18 KJV

**592.** I will see you again and then you will rejoice and no one can rob you of that joy.   John 16:22 LB

**593.** The righteous shall be glad in the Lord, and shall trust in him; and all the upright in heart shall glory.   Psalm 64:10 KJV

**594.** He heals the brokenhearted, binding up their wounds.   Psalm 147:3 LB

**595.** These things have I spoken unto you, that my joy might remain in you, and that your joy might be full.   John 15:11 KJV

**596.** The kingdom of God is not meat and drink; but righteousness, and peace, and joy in the Holy Ghost.   Romans 14:17 KJV

**597.** You love what is good and hate what is wrong. Therefore God, your God, has given you more gladness than anyone else.   Psalm 45:7 LB

**598.** Therefore you will joyously draw water from the springs of salvation.   Isaiah 12:3 NASB

**599.** You have let me experience the joys of life and the exquisite pleasures of your own eternal presence.   Psalm 16:11 LB

**600.** You love him even though you have never seen him; though not seeing him, you trust him; and even now you are happy with the inexpressible joy that comes from heaven itself.   I Peter 1:8 LB

**601.** Let the righteous be glad; let them exult before God; Yes, let them rejoice with gladness.   Psalm 68:3 NASB

**602.** You will go out with joy, and be led forth with peace.   Isaiah 55:12 NASB

**603.** He has given me a new song to sing, of praises to our God. Now many will hear of the glorious things he did for me, and stand in awe before the Lord, and put their trust in him. Psalm 40:3 LB

**604.** If you should suffer for the sake of righteousness, you are blessed. And do not fear their intimidation, and do not be troubled. I Peter 3:14 NASB

**605.** Happy the man who puts his trust in the Lord. Proverbs 16:20 LB

**606.** In thy name they rejoice all the day, and by thy righteousness they are exalted. Psalm 89:16 NASB

**607.** You shall rejoice in all the good which the Lord your God has given you and your household. Deuteronomy 26:11 NASB

**608.** Make everyone rejoice who puts his trust in you. Psalm 5:11 LB


# I. Do you need protection?

**KEY VERSE: 609.** *What's more, I am with you, and will protect you wherever you go.* Genesis 28:15 LB

**610.** I will lie down in peace and sleep, for though I am alone, O Lord, you will keep me safe. Psalm 4:8 LB

**611.** But all who listen to me shall live in peace and safety, unafraid. Proverbs 1:33 LB

**612.** The Lord is my light and my salvation. Whom shall I fear? The Lord is the strength of my life; of whom shall I be afraid? Psalm 27:1 KJV

**613.** The beloved of the Lord shall dwell in safety by him; and the Lord shall cover him all the day long. Deuteronomy 33:12 KJV

**614.** For he orders his angels to protect you wherever you go. Psalm 91:11 LB

**615.** The Lord is a strong fortress. The godly run to him and are safe. Proverbs 18:10 LB

**616.** I will say of the Lord, He is my refuge and my fortress: my God; in him will I trust.  Psalm 91:2 KJV

**617.** I know the one in whom I trust, and I am sure that he is able to safely guard all that I have given him until the day of his return.  II Timothy 1:12 LB

**618.** Though I walk in the midst of trouble, thou wilt revive me; thou wilt stretch forth thy hand against the wrath of my enemies, and thy right hand will save me.  Psalm 138:7 NASB

**619.** I will put you in the cleft of the rock and cover you with my hand until I have passed.  Exodus 33:22 LB

**620.** He who dwells in the shelter of the most high will abide in the shadow of the Almighty.  Psalm 91:1 NASB

**621.** And who is there to harm you if you prove zealous for what is good?  I Peter 3:13 NASB

**622.** As the mountains surround Jerusalem, so the Lord surrounds his people from this time forth and forever.  Psalm 125:2 NASB

**623.** The angel of the Lord guards and rescues all who reverence him.  Psalm 34:7 LB

**624.** When you go through deep waters and great trouble, I will be with you. When you go through rivers of difficulty, you will not drown! When you walk through the fire of oppression, you will not be burned up—the flames will not consume you.  Isaiah 43:2 LB

**625.** The good man does not escape all troubles—he has them too. But the Lord helps him in each and every one.  Psalm 34:19 LB

**626.** You are my hiding place from every storm of life; you even keep me from getting into trouble! You surround me with songs of victory.  Psalm 32:7 LB

**627.** Now I know that the Lord saves his anointed; he will answer him from his holy heaven, with the saving strength of his right hand.  Psalm 20:6 NASB

**628.** He fills me with strength and protects me wherever I go.   Psalm 18:32 LB

**629.** God is our refuge and strength, a very present help in trouble.   Psalm 46:1 KJV

# J. Is sickness a problem?

**KEY VERSE: 630.** *The prayer of faith shall save the sick, and the Lord shall raise him up.   James 5:15 KJV*

**631.** These signs shall follow them that believe; they shall lay hands on the sick, and they shall recover.   Mark 16:17,18 KJV

**632.** Admit your faults to one another and pray for each other so that you may be healed. The earnest prayer of a righteous man has great power and wonderful results.   James 5:16 LB

**633.** He was wounded for our transgressions, he was bruised for our iniquities: the chastisement of our peace was upon him; and with his stripes we are healed. Isaiah 53:5 KJV

**634.** I will give you back your health again and heal your wounds.   Jeremiah 30:17 LB

**635.** The Lord will remove from you all sickness; and he will not put on you any of the harmful diseases of Egypt which you have known.   Deuteronomy 7:15 NASB

**636.** The Lord will sustain him upon his sickbed; in his illness, thou dost restore him to health.   Psalm 41:3 NASB

**637.** Each time he said, "No. But I am with you; that is all you need. My power shows up best in weak people." Now I am glad to boast about how weak I am; I am glad to be a living demonstration of Christ's power, instead of showing off my own power and abilities.   II Corinthians 12:9 LB

**638.** These troubles and sufferings of ours are, after all, quite small and won't last very long. Yet this short time of distress will result in God's richest blessing upon us forever and ever.   II Corinthians 4:17 LB

**639.** Then your light will break out like the dawn, and your recovery will speedily spring forth; and your righteousness will go before you; the glory of the Lord will be your rear guard.   Isaiah 58:8 NASB

**640.** Yes, I will bless the Lord and not forget the glorious things he does for me. He forgives all my sins. He heals me.   Psalm 103:2,3 LB

**641.** You shall serve the Lord your God only; then I will bless you with food and with water, and I will take away sickness from among you.   Exodus 23:25 LB

**642.** I will bring it health and cure, and I will cure them, and will reveal unto them the abundance of peace and truth.   Jeremiah 33:6 KJV

**643.** O my soul, don't be discouraged. Don't be upset. Expect God to act! For I know that I shall again have plenty of reason to praise him for all that he will do. He is my help! He is my God!   Psalm 42:11 LB

**644.** I, the Lord, am your healer.   Exodus 15:26 NASB

**645.** Anything is possible if you have faith.   Mark 9:23 LB

**646.** He personally carried the load of our sins in his own body when he died on the cross, so that we can be finished with sin and live a good life from now on. For his wounds have healed ours!   I Peter 2:24 LB

# K. What about your friends?

**KEY VERSE: 647.** *Do not be deceived: "Bad company corrupts good morals."*   I Corinthians 15:33 NASB

**648.** When someone becomes a Christian he becomes a brand new person inside. He is not the same any more. A new life has begun! II Corinthians 5:17 LB

**649.** If we walk in the light, as he is in the light, we have fellowship one with another. I John 1:7 KJV

**650.** There are "friends" who pretend to be friends, but there is a friend who sticks closer than a brother. Proverbs 18:24 LB

**651.** No longer do I call you slaves; for the slave does not know what his master is doing; but I have called you friends, for all things that I have heard from my Father I have made known to you. John 15:15 NASB

**652.** Follow the steps of the godly instead, and stay on the right path. Proverbs 2:20 LB

**653.** Blessed is the man who does not walk in the counsel of the wicked, nor stand in the path of sinners, nor sit in the seat of scoffers! Psalm 1:1 NASB

**654.** A true friend is always loyal, and a brother is born to help in time of need. Proverbs 17:17 LB

**655.** Leave them; separate yourselves from them; don't touch their filthy things, and I will welcome you. II Corinthians 6:17 LB

**656.** Be with wise men and become wise. Be with evil men and become evil. Proverbs 13:20 LB

**657.** You are my friends, if you do what I command you. John 15:14 NASB

# L. Is a good reputation important?

**KEY VERSE: 658.** *A good name is rather to be chosen than great riches, and loving favor rather than silver and gold. Proverbs 22:1 KJV*

**659.** A good name is better than precious ointment.   Ecclesiastes 7:1 KJV

**660.** He will bring forth your righteousness as the light, and your judgment as the noonday.   Psalm 37:6 NASB

**661.** Be happy if you are cursed and insulted for being a Christian, for when that happens the Spirit of God will come upon you with great glory.   I Peter 4:14 LB

**662.** It is an honor for a man to stay out of a fight. Only fools insist on quarreling.   Proverbs 20:3 LB

**663.** You will be safe from slander; no need to fear the future.   Job 5:21 LB

**664.** He will send down help from heaven to save me, because of his love and his faithfulness.   Psalm 57:3 LB

**665.** Listen to me, you who know the right from the wrong and cherish my laws in your hearts: don't be afraid of people's scorn or their slanderous talk.   Isaiah 51:7 LB

**666.** Get rid of your sins and leave all iniquity behind you. Only then, without spots of sin to defile you, can you walk steadily forward to God without fear.   Job 11:14,15 LB

**667.** He who is slow to anger is better than the mighty, and he who rules his spirit, than he who captures a city.   Proverbs 16:32 NASB

**668.** Thou dost hide them in the secret place of thy presence from the conspiracies of man; thou dost keep them secretly in a shelter from the strife of tongues. Psalm 31:20 NASB

# M. Do you often feel insecure?

**KEY VERSE: 669.** *The eternal God is a dwelling place, and underneath are the everlasting arms.   Deuteronomy 33:27 NASB*

**670.** God is our refuge and strength, a very present help in trouble.   Psalm 46:1 KJV

**671.** In the fear of the Lord is strong confidence: and his children shall have a place of refuge.   Proverbs 14:26 KJV

**672.** The Lord is their strength, and he is the saving strength of his anointed.   Psalm 28:8 KJV

**673.** I can do all things through him who strengthens me.   Philippians 4:13 NASB

**674.** The Lord is a strong fortress. The godly run to him and are safe.   Proverbs 18:10 LB

**675.** To the poor, O Lord, you are a refuge from the storm, a shadow from the heat.   Isaiah 25:4 LB

**676.** When he falls, he shall not be hurled headlong; because the Lord is the one who holds his hand.   Psalm 37:24 NASB

**677.** Day by day the Lord observes the good deeds done by godly men, and gives them eternal rewards. Psalm 37:18 LB

**678.** The Lord also will be a refuge for the oppressed, a refuge in times of trouble.   Psalm 9:9 KJV

**679.** All those who know your mercy, Lord, will count on you for help. For you have never forsaken those who trust in you.   Psalm 9:10 LB

**680.** Because he loves me, I will rescue him; I will make him great because he trusts in my name.   Psalm 91:14 LB

**681.** If God is on our side, who can ever be against us?   Romans 8:31 LB

**682.** The Lord is my helper and I am not afraid of anything that mere man can do to me.   Hebrews 13:6 LB

**683.** For I am the Lord your God, who upholds your right hand, who says to you, Do not fear, I will help you.   Isaiah 41:13 NASB

# N. Do you need wisdom?

**KEY VERSE: 684.** *If any of you lacks wisdom, let him ask of God, who gives to all men generously and without reproach, and it will be given to him. James 1:5 NASB*

**685.** For God gives those who please him wisdom, knowledge, and joy.   Ecclesiastes 2:26 LB

**686.** How blessed is the man who finds wisdom, and the man who gains understanding.   Proverbs 3:13 NASB

**687.** He will teach us of his ways, and we will walk in his paths.   Isaiah 2:3 KJV

**688.** The wise in heart will be called discerning. Proverbs 16:21 NASB

**689.** I am the light of the world. So if you follow me, you won't be stumbling through the darkness, for living light will flood your path.   John 8:12 LB

**690.** Evil men understand not judgment: but they that seek the Lord understand all things.   Proverbs 28:5 KJV

**691.** For the Lord grants wisdom! His every word is a treasure of knowledge and understanding. He grants good sense to the godly—his saints.   Proverbs 2:6,7 LB

**692.** I will bless the Lord who counsels me.   Psalm 16:7 LB

**693.** A wise man will hear, and will increase learning; and a man of understanding shall attain unto wise counsels.   Proverbs 1:5 KJV

**694.** We know that the Son of God is come, and hath given us an understanding, that we may know him that is true, even his Son Jesus Christ.   I John 5:20 KJV

**695.** The fear of the Lord is the beginning of wisdom: and the knowledge of the holy is understanding. Proverbs 9:10 KJV

**696.** He who gets wisdom loves his own soul; he who keeps understanding will find good. Proverbs 19:8 NASB

**697.** The man who isn't a Christian can't understand and can't accept these thoughts from God, which the Holy Spirit teaches us. They sound foolish to him, because only those who have the Holy Spirit within them can understand what the Holy Spirit means. Others just can't take it in. But the spiritual man has insight into everything. I Corinthians 2:14,15 LB

**698.** In everything you do, put God first, and he will direct you and crown your efforts with success. Proverbs 3:6 LB

**699.** Wisdom is a fountain of life to those possessing it. Proverbs 16:22 LB

**700.** True wisdom and power are God's. He alone knows what we should do; he understands. Job 12:13 LB

**701.** The mouth of the righteous flows with wisdom. Proverbs 10:31 NASB

**702.** We know about these things because God has sent his Spirit to tell us, and his Spirit searches out and shows us all of God's deepest secrets. I Corinthians 2:10 LB

**703.** He who believes in him shall not be disappointed. I Peter 2:6 NASB


# O. Are you lonely?

**KEY VERSE: 704.** *I will never, never fail you nor forsake you. Hebrews 13:5 LB*

**705.** For the mountains may depart and the hills disappear, but my kindness shall not leave you. My promise of peace for you will never be broken, says the Lord who has mercy upon you.    Isaiah 54:10 LB

**706.** Truly our fellowship is with the Father, and with his Son Jesus Christ.  I John 1:3 KJV

**707.** There are "friends" who pretend to be friends, but there is a friend who sticks closer than a brother.  Proverbs 18:24 LB

**708.** Behold, I stand at the door and knock; if any man hear my voice and open the door, I will come in to him, and will sup with him, and he with me.  Revelation 3:20 KJV

**709.** Draw nigh to God, and he will draw nigh to you.  James 4:8 KJV

**710.** I am always thinking of the Lord; and because he is so near, I never need to stumble or to fall.  Psalm 16:8 LB

**711.** And he said, My presence shall go with you, and I will give you rest.  Exodus 33:14 NASB

**712.** I have loved you, O my people, with an everlasting love; with lovingkindness I have drawn you to me.  Jeremiah 31:3 LB

**713.** The Lord will not cast off his people, neither will he forsake his inheritance.  Psalm 94:14 KJV

**714.** I am the Lord, I have called you in righteousness. I will also hold you by the hand and watch over you. Isaiah 42:6 NASB

**715.** These things will I do unto them, and not forsake them.  Isaiah 42:16 KJV

**716.** The Lord loves justice and fairness; he will never abandon his people. They will be kept safe forever. Psalm 37:28 LB

**717.** I am come that they might have life, and that they might have it more abundantly.  John 10:10 KJV

**718.** When my father and my mother forsake me, then the Lord will take me up.  Psalm 27:10 KJV

**719.** I will not leave you comfortless: I will come to you.   John 14:18 KJV

# P. Are you impatient for things to happen?

**KEY VERSE: 720.** *You need to keep on patiently doing God's will if you want him to do for you all that he has promised.   Hebrews 10:36 LB*

**721.** By your perseverance you will win your souls. Luke 21:19 NASB

**722.** And let us not get tired of doing what is right, for after a while we will reap a harvest of blessing if we don't get discouraged and give up.   Galatians 6:9 LB

**723.** There is an appointed time for everything. And there is a time for every event under heaven. Ecclesiastes 3:1 NASB

**724.** Rest in the Lord; wait patiently for him to act. Don't be envious of evil men who prosper. For the wicked shall be destroyed, but those who trust in the Lord shall be given every blessing.   Psalm 37:7,9 LB

**725.** When the way is rough, your patience has a chance to grow.   James 1:3 LB

**726.** When your patience is finally in full bloom, then you will be ready for anything, strong in character, full and complete.   James 1:4 LB

**727.** Now the God of patience and consolation grant you to be likeminded one toward another according to Christ Jesus.   Romans 15:5 KJV

**728.** Remain faithful even when facing death and I will give you the crown of life—an unending, glorious future.   Revelation 2:10 LB

**729.** Better is the end of a thing than the beginning

thereof: and the patient in spirit is better than the proud in spirit.   Ecclesiastes 7:8 KJV

**730.** Blessed is a man who perseveres under trial; for once he has been approved, he will receive the crown of life, which the Lord has promised to those who love him.   James 1:12 NASB

**731.** All of you who endure to the end shall be saved.   Matthew 10:22 LB

**732.** Behold, we count those blessed who endured. You have heard of the endurance of Job and have seen the outcome of the Lord's dealings, that the Lord is full of compassion and is merciful.   James 5:11 NASB

**733.** I waited patiently for the Lord; and he inclined unto me, and heard my cry.   Psalm 40:1 KJV

**734.** Do not throw away your confidence, which has a great reward. For yet a very little while, he who is coming will come, and will not delay.   Hebrews 10:35,37 NASB

**735.** And it shall be said in that day, Lo, this is our God; we have waited for him, we will be glad and rejoice in his salvation.   Isaiah 25:9 KJV

**736.** He is a rewarder of them that diligently seek him.   Hebrews 11:6 KJV

**737.** We can rejoice, too, when we run into problems and trials for we know that they are good for us—they help us learn to be patient. And patience develops strength of character in us and helps us trust God more each time we use it until finally our hope and faith are strong and steady.   Romans 5:3,4 LB

**738.** Don't be impatient. Wait for the Lord, and he will come and save you.   Psalm 27:14 LB

**739.** God has made an everlasting covenant with me; his agreement is eternal, final, sealed. He will constantly look after my safety and success.   II Samuel 23:5 LB

**740.** The effective prayer of a righteous man can accomplish much.   James 5:16 NASB

**741.** They that wait upon the Lord shall renew their strength; they shall mount up with wings as eagles; they shall run, and not be weary; and they shall walk, and not faint.   Isaiah 40:31 KJV

## Q. What if you are persecuted by others?

**KEY VERSE: 742.** *Blessed are they which are persecuted for righteousness' sake; for their's is the kingdom of heaven.   Matthew 5:10 KJV*

**743.** If we suffer, we shall also reign with him.   II Timothy 2:12 KJV

**744.** If you cling to your life, you will lose it; but if you give it up for me, you will save it.   Matthew 10:39 LB

**745.** Don't be bewildered or surprised when you go through the fiery trials ahead, for this is no strange, unusual thing that is going to happen to you. Instead, be really glad—because these trials will make you partners with Christ in his suffering, and afterwards you will have the wonderful joy of sharing his glory in that coming day when it will be displayed.   I Peter 4:12,13 LB

**746.** Be happy if you are cursed and insulted for being a Christian, for when that happens the Spirit of God will come upon you with great glory.   I Peter 4:14 LB

**747.** Do not say, "I will repay evil"; wait for the Lord, and he will save you.   Proverbs 20:22 NASB

**748.** Pardon, and you will be pardoned.   Luke 6:37 NASB

**749.** Blessed are the meek for they shall inherit the earth.   Matthew 5:5 KJV

**750.** Love your enemies! Pray for those who persecute you! In that way you will be acting as true sons of your father in heaven.   Matthew 5:44,45 LB

**751.** If your enemy is hungry, give him food! If he is thirsty, give him something to drink! This will make him feel ashamed of himself, and God will reward you.   Proverbs 25:21,22 LB

**752.** The Lord your God fights for you, just as he has promised.   Joshua 23:10 LB

**753.** You provide delicious food for me in the presence of my enemies. You have welcomed me as your guest; blessings overflow!   Psalm 23:5 LB

**754.** Make everyone rejoice who puts his trust in you. Keep them shouting for joy because you are defending them.   Psalm 5:11 LB

**755.** The eternal God is your refuge, and underneath are the everlasting arms. He thrusts out your enemies before you; it is he who cries, Destroy them!   Deuteronomy 33:27 LB

**756.** He gives justice to all who are treated unfairly.   Psalm 103:6 LB

**757.** For the Lord your God is the one who goes with you, to fight for you against your enemies, to save you.   Deuteronomy 20:4 NASB

**758.** Though I am surrounded by troubles, you will bring me safely through them. You will clench your fist against my angry enemies! Your power will save me.   Psalm 138:7 LB

**759.** He will keep the feet of his saints, and the wicked shall be silent in darkness; for by strength shall no man prevail.   I Samuel 2:9 KJV

**760.** The Lord your God is in your midst, a victorious warrior. He will exult over you with joy, he will be quiet in his love, he will rejoice over you with shouts of joy.   Zephaniah 3:17 NASB

**761.** The Lord will defeat your enemies before you;

they will march out together against you but scatter before you in seven directions. Deuteronomy 28:7 LB

**762.** God will not reject a man of integrity, nor will he support the evildoers. He will yet fill your mouth with laughter, and your lips with shouting. Job 8:20,21 NASB

**763.** The Lord opens the eyes of the blind; the Lord raises up those who are bowed down. Psalm 146:8 NASB

**764.** Give your burdens to the Lord. He will carry them. He will not permit the godly to slip or fall. Psalm 55:22 LB

**765.** For just as the sufferings of Christ are ours in abundance, so also our comfort is abundant through Christ. II Corinthians 1:5 NASB

**766.** We are troubled on every side, yet not distressed; we are perplexed, but not in despair; persecuted, but not forsaken; cast down, but not destroyed. II Corinthians 4:8,9 KJV

**767.** These things I have spoken to you, that in me you may have peace. In the world you have tribulation, but take courage; I have overcome the world. John 16:33 NASB

# R. Are you grieving over something?

**KEY VERSE: 768.** *Even when walking through the dark valley of death I will not be afraid, for you are close beside me, guarding, guiding all the way. Psalm 23:4 LB.*

**769.** May our Lord Jesus Christ himself and God our Father, who has loved us and given us everlasting comfort and hope which we don't deserve, comfort your hearts with all comfort, and help you in every good thing you say and do.   II Thessalonians 2:16,17 LB

**770.** When my anxious thoughts multiply within me, thy consolations delight my soul.   Psalm 94:19 NASB

**771.** The Lord has comforted his people, and will have compassion upon them in their sorrow.   Isaiah 49:13 LB

**772.** What a wonderful God we have—he is the Father of our Lord Jesus Christ, the source of every mercy, and the one who so wonderfully comforts and strengthens us in our hardships and trials. And why does he do this? So that when others are troubled, needing our sympathy and encouragement, we can pass on to them this same help and comfort God has given us.   II Corinthians 1:3,4 LB

**773.** I, even I, am he who comforts you.   Isaiah 51:12 NASB

**774.** It is the blessing of the Lord that makes rich, and he adds no sorrow to it.   Proverbs 10:22 NASB

**775.** This is my comfort in my affliction, that thy word has revived me.   Psalm 119:50 NASB

**776.** Blessed are they that mourn: for they shall be comforted.   Matthew 5:4 KJV

**777.** He knows the number of hairs on your head! Never fear, you are far more valuable to him than a whole flock of sparrows.   Luke 12:7 LB

**778.** The Lord has anointed me to bring good news to the suffering and afflicted. He has sent me to comfort the broken-hearted, to announce liberty to captives and to open the eyes of the blind. He has sent me to tell those who mourn that the time of God's favor to them has come. To all who mourn in Israel he will give: Beauty for ashes; joy instead of mourning; praise instead of heaviness.   Isaiah 61:1,2,3 LB

**779.** I will not leave you comfortless: I will come to you.   John 14:18 KJV

**780.** Only then, without the spots of sin to defile you, can you forget your misery. It will all be in the past.   Job 11:15,16 LB

**781.** The Lord is near to the brokenhearted, and saves those who are crushed in spirit.   Psalm 34:18 NASB

**782.** Comfort, oh, comfort my people, says your God.   Isaiah 40:1 LB

**783.** We know that all things work together for good to them that love God, to them who are the called according to his purpose.   Romans 8:28 KJV

**784.** It is a broken spirit you want—remorse and penitence. A broken and a contrite heart, O God, you will not ignore.   Psalm 51:17 LB

**785.** I will look with pity on the man who has a humble and a contrite heart, who trembles at my word.   Isaiah 66:2 LB

**786.** He heals the brokenhearted, binding up their wounds.   Psalm 147:3 LB


# S. Do you often feel inadequate or frustrated?

**KEY VERSE: 787.** *Surely, shall one say, in the Lord have I righteousness and strength.   Isaiah 45:24 KJV*

**788.** Of his fulness have all we received, and grace for grace. For the law was given by Moses, but grace and truth came by Jesus Christ.   John 1:16,17 KJV

**789.** But by his doing you are in Christ Jesus, who became to us wisdom from God, and righteousness and sanctification, and redemption.   I Corinthians 1:30 NASB

**790.** Unto us a child is born, unto us a son is given: and the government shall be upon his shoulder: and his name shall be called Wonderful, Counselor, The mighty God, The everlasting Father, The Prince of Peace.   Isaiah 9:6 KJV

**791.** Because I live, you shall live also.   John 14:19 NASB

**792.** I have been crucified with Christ; and it is no longer I who live, but Christ lives in me; and the life which I now live in the flesh I live by faith in the Son of God, who loved me, and delivered himself up for me.   Galatians 2:20 NASB

**793.** Commit everything you do to the Lord. Trust him to help you do it and he will.   Psalm 37:5 LB

**794.** He is able to save forever those who draw near to God through him, since he always lives to make intercession for them.   Hebrews 7:25 NASB

**795.** They are like trees along a river bank bearing luscious fruit each season without fail. Their leaves shall never wither, and all they do shall prosper.   Psalm 1:3 LB

**796.** He who has the Son has the life.   I John 5:12 NASB

**797.** Overwhelming victory is ours through Christ who loved us enough to die for us.   Romans 8:37 LB

**798.** Everyone can see how much he loves me. His left hand is under my head and with his right hand he embraces me.   Song of Solomon 2:4,6 LB

**799.** You hath he quickened, who were dead in trespasses and sins, and hath raised us up together, and made us sit together in heavenly places.   Ephesians 2:1,6 KJV

**800.** When someone wants to do wrong it is never God who is tempting him, for God never wants to do wrong and never tempts anyone else to do it.   James 1:13 LB

**801.** Let us therefore come boldly unto the throne of grace, that we may obtain mercy, and find grace to help in time of need.   Hebrews 4:16 KJV

*Beloved, now are we*
*the sons of God, and*
*it doth not yet appear*
*what we shall be: but*
*we know that, when he shall*
*appear, we shall be like him;*
*for we shall see him as he is.*
*I John 3:2 (KJV)*

# GOD'S PROMISES FOR YOUR FUTURE NEEDS

## A. What does the future hold? The return of Jesus Christ!

**KEY VERSE: 802.** *Looking for that blessed hope, and the glorious appearing of the great God and our Saviour Jesus Christ.   Titus 2:13 KJV*

**803.** For the Lord himself will descend from heaven with a shout, with the voice of the archangel, and with the trumpet of God.   I Thessalonians 4:16 NASB

**804.** They shall see the Son of man coming in the clouds of heaven with power and great glory.   Matthew 24:30 KJV

**805.** Remember what I told you—I am going away, but I will come back to you again.   John 14:28 LB

**806.** So be prepared, for you don't know what day your Lord is coming.   Matthew 24:42 LB

**807.** I know that my redeemer lives, and at the last he will take his stand on the earth.   Job 19:25 NASB

**808.** And his feet shall stand in that day upon the Mount of Olives, which is before Jerusalem.   Zechariah 14:4 KJV

**809.** Behold, he is coming with the clouds, and every eye will see him, even those who pierced him.   Revelation 1:7 NASB

**810.** The Lord direct your hearts into the love of God, and into the patient waiting for Christ.   II Thessalonians 3:5 KJV

**811.** When Christ, who is our life, is revealed, then you also will be revealed with him in glory.   Colossians 3:4 NASB

**812.** We know that, when he shall appear, we shall be like him; for we shall see him as he is.   I John 3:2 KJV

**813.** You shall see the Son of man sitting at the right hand of power, and coming with the clouds of heaven.   Mark 14:62 NASB

**814.** So Christ was once offered to bear the sins of many; and unto them that look for him shall he appear the second time without sin unto salvation.   Hebrews 9:28 KJV

**815.** Awaiting eagerly the revelation of our Lord Jesus Christ, who shall also confirm you to the end, blameless in the day of our Lord Jesus Christ.   I Corinthians 1:7,8 NASB

**816.** Judge nothing before the time, until the Lord come, who both will bring to light the hidden things of darkness, and will make manifest the counsels of the hearts.   I Corinthians 4:5 KJV

**817.** They shall look upon me whom they have pierced, and they shall mourn for him.   Zechariah 12:10 KJV

**818.** As often as you eat this bread and drink the cup, you proclaim the Lord's death until he comes.   I Corinthians 11:26 NASB

**819.** You too, be ready; for the Son of man is coming at an hour that you do not expect.   Luke 12:40 NASB

**820.** There shall come in the last days scoffers, walking after their own lusts, and saying, Where is the promise of his coming? For since the fathers fell asleep, all things continue as they were from the beginning of the creation. But the day of the Lord will come as a thief in the night.   II Peter 3:3,4,10 KJV

**821.** Blessed are those servants, whom the Lord when he cometh shall find watching.   Luke 12:37 KJV

**822.** Just as the lightning comes from the east, and flashes even to the west, so shall the coming of the Son of man be.   Matthew 24:27 NASB

**823.** This Jesus, who has been taken up from you into heaven, will come in just the same way as you have watched him go into heaven.   Acts 1:11 NASB

# B. There will be a great resurrection of the dead in Christ.

**KEY VERSE: 824.** *The trumpet shall sound, and the dead shall be raised incorruptible, and we shall be changed.   I Corinthians 15:52 KJV*

**825.** The dead in Christ shall rise first. Then we who are alive and remain shall be caught up together with them in the clouds to meet the Lord in the air, and thus we shall always be with the Lord.   I Thessalonians 4:16,17 NASB

**826.** An hour is coming, in which all who are in the tombs shall hear his voice, and shall come forth.   John 5:28,29 NASB

**827.** So when this corruptible shall have put on incorruption, and this mortal shall have put on immortality, then shall be brought to pass the saying that is written,

Death is swallowed up in victory.   I Corinthians 15:54 KJV

**828.** Thanks be to God, who gives us the victory through our Lord Jesus Christ.   I Corinthians 15:57 NASB

**829.** This is the will of my Father, that every one who beholds the Son, and believes in him, may have eternal life, and I myself will raise him up on the last day.   John 6:40 NASB

**830.** And if the Spirit of God, who raised up Jesus from the dead, lives in you, he will make your dying bodies live again after you die, by means of this same Holy Spirit living within you.   Romans 8:11 LB

**831.** Just as each of us now has a body like Adam's, so we shall some day have a body like Christ's.   I Corinthians 15:49 LB

**832.** Since by man came death, by man came also the resurrection of the dead. For as in Adam all die, even so in Christ shall all be made alive.   I Corinthians 15:21,22 KJV

**833.** I am the resurrection, and the life; he who believes in me shall live even if he dies.   John 11:25 NASB

**834.** This is the will of God, that I should not lose even one of all those he has given me, but that I should raise them to eternal life at the last day.   John 6:39 LB

**835.** Our Savior Christ Jesus, who abolished death, and brought life and immortality to light through the gospel.   II Timothy 1:10 NASB

**836.** Since we believe that Jesus died and then came back to life again, we can also believe that when Jesus returns, God will bring back with him all the Christians who have died.   I Thessalonians 4:14 LB

**837.** He who raised the Lord Jesus will raise us also with Jesus and will present us with you.   II Corinthians 4:14 NASB

# C. You will receive heavenly rewards.

**KEY VERSE: 838.** *In my Father's house are many mansions: if it were not so, I would have told you. I go to prepare a place for you. And if I go and prepare a place for you, I will come again, and receive you unto myself; that where I am, there ye may be also. John 14:2,3 KJV*

**839.** According to his promise we are looking for new heavens and a new earth, in which righteousness dwells. II Peter 3:13 NASB

**840.** There is laid up for me a crown of righteousness, which the Lord, the righteous judge, shall give me at that day; and not to me only, but unto all them also that love his appearing. II Timothy 4:8 KJV

**841.** There will be no night there—no need for lamps or sun—for the Lord God will be their light; and they shall reign forever and ever. Revelation 22:5 LB

**842.** They desire a better country, that is a heavenly one. Therefore God is not ashamed to be called their God; for he has prepared a city for them. Hebrews 11:16 NASB

**843.** So shall we ever be with the Lord. I Thessalonians 4:17 KJV

**844.** They are before the throne of God, and serve him day and night in his temple; and he that sitteth on the throne shall dwell among them. Revelation 7:15 KJV

**845.** They shall hunger no more, neither thirst any more; neither shall the sun beat down on them, nor any heat. Revelation 7:16 NASB

**846.** For the Lamb in the center of the throne shall be their shepherd, and shall guide them to springs of the water of life; and God shall wipe every tear from their eyes. Revelation 7:17 NASB

**847.** Remain faithful even when facing death and I will give you the crown of life—an unending, glorious future.   Revelation 2:10 LB

**848.** As for me, I will behold thy face in righteousness; I shall be satisfied, when I awake, with thy likeness. Psalm 17:15 KJV

**849.** Then the godly shall shine as the sun in their Father's kingdom.   Matthew 13:43 LB

**850.** When Christ, who is our life, is revealed, then you also will be revealed with him in glory.   Colossians 3:4 NASB

**851.** His lord said unto him, Well done, thou good and faithful servant: thou hast been faithful over a few things, I will make thee ruler over many things: enter thou into the joy of thy lord.   Matthew 25:21 KJV

**852.** Come, you who are blessed of my Father, inherit the kingdom prepared for you from the foundation of the world.   Matthew 25:34 NASB

**853.** Treasures in heaven, where neither moth nor rust destroys, and where thieves do not break in or steal.   Matthew 6:20 NASB

**854.** I appoint unto you a kingdom, as my Father hath appointed unto me; that ye may eat and drink at my table in my kingdom, and sit on thrones judging the twelve tribes of Israel.   Luke 22:29,30 KJV

**855.** Blessed be the God and Father of our Lord Jesus Christ, who according to his great mercy has caused us to be born again to a living hope through the resurrection of Jesus Christ from the dead, to obtain an inheritance which is imperishable and undefiled and will not fade away, reserved in heaven for you.   I Peter 1:3,4 NASB

**856.** What we suffer now is nothing compared to the glory he will give us later.   Romans 8:18 LB

**857.** For the Son of man shall come in the glory of his Father with his angels; and then he shall reward every man according to his works.    Matthew 16:27 KJV

**858.** No mere man has ever seen, heard or even imagined what wonderful things God has ready for those who love the Lord.  I Corinthians 2:9 LB

**859.** And when the chief Shepherd shall appear, ye shall receive a crown of glory that fadeth not away.  I Peter 5:4 KJV

**860.** He who overcomes shall inherit these things, and I will be his God and he will be my son.  Revelation 21:7 NASB

**861.** He will wipe away all tears from their eyes, and there shall be no more death, nor sorrow, nor crying, nor pain. All of that has gone forever.    Revelation 21:4 LB

**862.** He who overcomes, I will grant to him to sit down with me on my throne, as I also overcame and sat down with my Father on his throne.   Revelation 3:21 NASB

**863.** After these things I looked, and behold, a great multitude, which no one could count, from every nation and all tribes and peoples and tongues, standing before the throne and before the Lamb, clothed in white robes, and palm branches were in their hands.    Revelation 7:9 NASB

**864.** Well done, good and faithful servant; thou hast been faithful over a few things, I will make thee ruler over many things: enter thou into the joy of thy Lord.    Matthew 25:23 KJV

**865.** Blessed are they that do his commandments, that they may have right to the tree of life, and may enter in through the gates into the city.   Revelation 22:14 KJV

**866.** Behold, I come quickly; and my reward is with me, to give every man according as his work shall be.   Revelation 22:12 KJV

**867.** He which testifieth these things said, Surely I come quickly. Amen. Even so, come, Lord Jesus.   Revelation 22:20 KJV